FLAVOR
EXPOSED

# FLAVOR EXPOSED

## 100 GLOBAL RECIPES
## FROM SWEET TO SALTY
## EARTHY TO SPICY

ANGELO SOSA

WITH SUZANNE LENZER

Photography by
William Brinson

**Dedication**
For my son Jacob. Follow your dreams, for they will come true.

Published in 2012 by Kyle Books, an imprint of Kyle Cathie Limited. www.kylebooks.com

Distributed by National Book Network, 4501 Forbes Blvd, Suite 200, Lanham, MD 20706
Phone: (800) 462-6420
Fax: (301) 429-5746
custserv@nbnbooks.com

ISBN 978-1-906868-66-6

10 9 8 7 6 5 4 3 2 1

**Design** Nicky Collings
**Photography** William Brinson
**Project editor** Anja Schmidt
**Food stylist** Adrienne Anderson
**Props stylist** Paige Hicks
**Copy editor** Leda Scheintaub
**Production** Gemma John and Nic Jones

Library of Congress Control No: 2011945816

Color reproduction by Scanhouse
Printed and bound in China

# Contents

# Foreword | By Alain Ducasse

Don't expect me to tell you that Angelo Sosa is an excellent chef. There's no use in stating the obvious: any food lover who has followed Angelo's career over the last ten years has had the opportunity to see (and ideally taste) tangible evidence of his talent in all the restaurants where he has worked. And the ones who missed these opportunities now hold in their hands this book, a collection which showcases Angelo's knowhow.

Besides, saying that Angelo Sosa is a great chef would miss a crucial point. I believe he is one of the most accomplished examples of what contemporary cuisine is all about. As Angelo kindly reminds me, I had a big shock when, by chance, I myself ate at Yumcha. As the restaurant had an open kitchen, I witnessed in detail how Angelo was working; the precision of his gestures and his impeccable organization.

More importantly though is Angelo's insatiable curiosity. His eyes are constantly wide open onto the world. His passion for Asian flavors is well known; something he nourished with Jean-Georges Vongerichten and which eventually led him to travel Asia, from Hong Kong to Korea to Vietnam; these experiences irrigate this book. As a result, he is equally capable of delivering a high-end version of this Asian cuisine he loves so much as well as rustic, more casual interpretation. He knows how to be faithful to this inspiration yet how to incorporate various other influences to satisfy Western, urban palates. Angelo has mastered his art so well that he can juggle all these varied elements and never fall into the trap of creating "confusion food." His cuisine is always clear, straightforward.

This mix of technical perfection and passion comes from Angelo's strong personality. Coupled with his elegant approach, Angelo's cuisine is utterly unique. One can feel his passion for Asian flavors, his talent for combining them harmoniously, and his uninhibited creativity in each and every of his recipes. They all tell a story—the story of a chef who lives for cooking.

# Introduction

One of the most awesome moments in my career was a very quiet one. Picture this: I'm meeting with Jean-Georges Vongerichten about a job at his four-star restaurant in New York City. The interview has just begun, when, in his heavy French accent, he says simply, "Follow me," and leads me into his kitchen for the first time. As I remember it, everything was brilliantly white and silver, utterly clean, and nearly silent, except for the metallic clinking of a few pans, the hollow sound of copper against copper. That room, at that moment, was what I imagine heaven must be like; gleaming surfaces and rich, exotic aromas surrounding me. In a hushed voice, Jean-Georges said, "Watch," and put his hand on the handle of the Bonnet oven door to pull it open—I stood there wide-eyed and in awe. I'd never seen a Bonnet before. Then he put my hand on the handle and he let go. The weight of it was intense—it felt like ten pounds of metal in my fist. I could see my reflection in the stainless steel surrounding the open door, could feel the heat emanating from inside and wafting around my head. It was beautiful—what more can I say?

From that moment on I was totally seduced, not just by the cool-factor of that stunning oven, but also by the food I was cooking and everything I was learning as I worked side-by-side with Jean-Georges. As the ultimate perfectionist, he taught me the importance of never compromising, of never settling for good enough. It's because of Jean-Georges that I have the work ethic I have; it's also because of him that I developed the philosophy that I live and work by. The belief that simplicity is complexity, that stripping things down to their bare essence, their purest form, is what it's all about.

Jean-Georges's food, while inspired by the four-star cuisine of France, is heavily influenced by Asian flavors and relies on many ingredients completely unorthodox—if not totally unheard of—in traditional French cooking. During the years that I worked with him I discovered an entirely new world of flavors and innovative ways of combining them—green apples with endive, raw fish with grape jelly, lamb crusted with black trumpet mushrooms. Jean-Georges is like that, he's a mad scientist when it comes to flavor combinations. After working with him, I realized I had to go to Asia for myself, to grow as a chef and a person. I needed to taste these exotic ingredients at their most authentic, and I wanted to submerge myself in the culture whose food had totally captivated me. Talk about a trip that rocked my world.

# A Mind-Blowing Journey into the World of Flavors

**Traveling through Asia** I was enamored by the incredible range of herbs, spices, and ingredients all around me. But at the same time I seriously felt like I was home, like I'd found my place in the world. I remember walking through a market in Hanoi one day, the air was steamy and thick with that fertile scent of produce just out of the fields—vegetables of all shapes, colors, and sizes with damp earth still clinging to their skin. I recall standing there, in the chaos of chattering animals and bartering shoppers, thinking, "What is this smell that's drawing me in?" Then it hit me: saw-tooth coriander—musty, aggressive, and way more edgy in flavor than cilantro. I picked up a bunch and just stood there, totally lost in my own world thinking, "How do I use this? How do I pull out the essence of this herb?"

Then I noticed a wooden box full of lemongrass stalks, plump at one end and stiff as bamboo at the other, and I couldn't help myself. I picked up one of the stalks and whacked it, literally smashed it against the side of the box. There was a serious "thwack!" sound as the stalk split, and the bright, acidic aroma spilled out into the air. The man who was selling the lemongrass looked at me as though I was out of my mind, but I was so caught up in that vibrant fragrance that I barely noticed. I was already fantasizing about how that lemongrass would work with the coriander, and wouldn't those flavors be great with fish and some sort of a salty-sweet caramel sauce with a kick of curry . . .

### Breaking It Down, Bringing Flavor to Life

This is how it is when I'm coming up with new dishes: I get obsessed by a flavor, an ingredient, a taste, and I begin to pair it up with other complementary flavors. Then I decide which ingredients mesh well with these flavors. Most of my food is based on a trinity of flavors; the idea is that to create a dish that really works you need three different components that are the key focal points. Let's say I start with sweet, salty, smoky. Think of bacon and eggs. You have the smoky, salty bacon and you jazz up the eggs with some sweet ketchup. Right there you've got your trinity of flavors. Now think about chorizo and onions, smoked salmon and pickles, prosciutto and grilled watermelon. These are all based on exactly the same flavor combo, one that we're totally familiar with—all I do is up the ante by using unexpected ingredients. And you can push it even further—if you want live lavish, how about adding a nice thin slice of red snapper to that prosciutto and watermelon?

In this book I focus on nine core flavor profiles: sweet, salty, smoky, bitter, sour, umami, spicy, earthy, and nutty (see Flavor Map on pages 12 to 13). But there are many other flavor profiles in addition to these (think acidic, herbaceous, astringent, floral, and more). That's why in addition to placing each recipe under a main flavor chapter, I also provide a note about the more subtle trinity of flavors within that specific dish. Consider my Sweet Tomato Soup with Curried Whipped Cream: This dish is included in the Sweet chapter because the foremost flavor—the flavor that initiated its development—is the sweet tomatoes. But I've also categorized it as astringent and spicy—this is because not only do the tomatoes have a hint of acid to them, but the garlic and ginger have a definite astringency that while subtle is very present. The gochujang paste and the curry offer a distinctly spicy element that's also an essential part of the final dish. So while the main flavor is sweet, there are secondary flavors that make up the trinity—and make the dish more complex and vibrant when you taste it.

Bonito

**Smoky**

Smoked
bacon

Chorizo

Chipotle

Sugar

Watermelon

Lychee

**Sweet**

Gula melaka

White chocolate

Pineapple

Maple syrup

Flav

Wasabi

Ginger

Sambal

Sancho pepper

Sriracha

**Spicy**

Gochujang

Thai chile

Kimchi

Jalapeño

Sesame seeds

Basmati rice

Almonds

**Nutty**

Coriander seed

Cashews

Toasted
sesame oil

Mustard seed

# Map

## Salty
Salt

Oyster sauce

Fish sauce

Soy sauce

Shrimp paste

## Earthy
Truffle

Black peppercorns

Tomatoes

arsnip

Turkish pepper

Black cardamon

Beets

Unsweetened cocoa powder

Turmeric

## Umami
Soy sauce

Shrimp paste

Tomatoes

Shiitake mushrooms

Pancetta

## Bitter
Iceberg lettuce

Mustard seed

Wasabi

Frisée

Oolong tea

Cumin seed

## Sour
Lemon

Seasoned rice wine vinegar

Tamarind

Pineapple

Yuzu

# We Are Extractors

As chefs and home cooks, we have to think of ourselves as extractors—our job is to find ways to pull the essence out of each ingredient to let their individual nuances shine. For example, I always try to extract the essential oils from herbs and spices to get the most out of them. With fresh herbs, I crush or smash them to release the oils (for example, lemongrass stalks are usually smashed and then chopped and rosemary or thyme is usually crushed or massaged).

When it comes to spices, I almost always start with whole spices. Then I follow a very simple but essential process for extracting the most flavor: I toast them low and slow until just aromatic, let them cool thoroughly, and then grind them in a spice grinder (a coffee grinder I use only for spices). This may seem labor intensive, but it's really not; in fact, you can toast all the spices you need for a recipe in one skillet—just start with the largest ones first and add the others as each begins to release its fragrance. Be sure to add them in descending order of size until they are all aromatic. (Always cool the spices before grinding them; if they're hot, the volatile oils will stick to the grinder and you'll lose that vibrant aromatic flavor.)

Extraction is all about using techniques to combine ingredients to create a totally balanced, harmonious relationship. Maybe it's on the wok, where the high heat and energy is like standing in front of a 747 jet—fast and furious. Maybe we treat food like a tea and let it steep, slowly and gently, to release its essence. Or maybe we pickle an ingredient, allowing other flavors to penetrate and enhance it. There are many different techniques that respect the integrity of our ingredients and can be used in the pursuit of flavor, but the end goal is always the same: To bring out the best in the finest ingredients and never lose sight of the fact that it's about the y-factor (yummy-factor). It's about making food that's not just transporting, but transcendent.

### Aiming for the Fences

In my career, one of the things I've become known for is my ability to combine ingredients that are seemingly at odds with one another in tantalizing ways. I believe I have a heightened sense of flavor that helps me in this capacity (I think this is partially something I was born with but also something that my parents helped me develop from a very early age by introducing me to adventurous foods). But this ability is something we all have access to—we just have to learn how to develop it.

I have this dish I made on Top Chef that's a great example: I take fish and marinate it in turmeric and put it with a cilantro and dill salad. Then I add some smoky chorizo, and then, wait for it . . . I grate white chocolate over the top. Now I totally admit, this is not a simple weeknight dinner (even for me!), but it works because the balance of all these different flavors are perfectly aligned: the herbaceous dill, the smoky chorizo, and the sweet chocolate. After tasting this dish, David Chang, one of the guest judges, said, "Man, you just swung for the fences," and he was right. I knew when I served that dish that I'd nailed it—but the truth is, that dish was a leap for me. Yes, I was used to mixing flavors in unexpected ways, but the whole Top Chef experience pushed me to go even further, to expand my own boundaries, and to think beyond the flavor combinations I was comfortable with. It made me a more daring chef. And that's exactly what I want to help you do with this book; I want you to push the limits of your own comfort zone, to begin a more adventurous relationship with food. I want to encourage you to attempt more audacious combinations in your own cooking, to help you look at recipes and food from a different perspective, to break dishes down into flavor profiles, and ultimately, to have more fun in the kitchen and at the dinner table.

Look, I'm not suggesting that you start serving curried caviar and chocolate for dinner (though it's a killer combo, so why not?), but you can learn how to enhance your cooking by understanding the expansive world of flavor and how it works. Wine is a great example: When you swish the wine around in the glass and you smell it, that first sense you experience is the fragrance, the bouquet, the aroma—that scent that teases your taste buds as to what's yet to come. Next is that first sip, when you begin to savor the taste and categorize those abundant flavors more clearly: blackberries, chocolate, citrus, maybe a touch of vanilla. Then your mind begins to put those familiar flavors into broader categories: sweet, bitter, earthy, smoky. What you're doing with wine is discerning the different tastes—and this is exactly what I'm suggesting you do with food—begin to think about flavors that work together, and then how various ingredients imbued with these flavors can be combined. Yes, it's a different and slightly more sophisticated way to contemplate dinner, but it's sexy and seductive too.

Listen, we eat every day, for our entire lives. Shouldn't our food, our sustenance, be as exciting as possible? I think so. And I think that with a bit of knowledge and some guidance anyone can cook something that awakens the senses and enhances daily life—or just tastes absolutely delicious.

## Sources
Many of the ingredients I use can be found at traditional grocery stores in the international food section. I personally shop at small Asian markets for some specialty items though I buy the majority of my products at Kalustyan's in New York City. Their store is an amazing emporium of spices, exotic herbs, sauces, grains, breads, and more. They have a fabulous online store as well: kalustyans.com.

Kalustyan's
123 Lexington Avenue
New York, NY 10016
1-800-352-3451

Sweet Tomato Soup with Curried Whipped Cream

# Scallop and Banana Tartare with Jalapeño Vinaigrette

Chilled Ramen Noodles with Watermelon Tea

# Grilled Duck Breast with Honey-Pepper Glaze

Saigon Burgers with Ginger Glaze and Thai Basil Mayo

# Braised Short Ribs with Lemongrass Honey

Slow-Cooked Asian Pork Belly

# Roasted Butternut Squash with Spiced Caramel

Grilled Corn with Sweet Coconut Flakes and Spicy Mayo

# Shaved Ice with Green Tea Syrup and Fruity Pebbles

Vanilla Bean and Cardamom Tapioca Pudding

# Chocolate Brownie with Gula Melaka Toffee and Chai Milkshake

Turmeric-Onion Jam

# Candied Ginger and Juniper Breadcrumbs

Curried White Chocolate Sauce

# Sweet

# Sweet | My inspiration

**Before I'd even step over her threshold,** I could hear the sizzling, the cracking and popping of hot oil in a pan. I was too young to know the smells or to name them—bay leaf, cilantro, chile, cumin, oregano—but they'd envelop me; I wanted to eat the air. My Aunt Carmen's kitchen in Queens, New York, was my salvation as a child. While my sisters and cousins would be outside playing, I would drag a stool across the kitchen, scramble up, and sit, mesmerized as she turned the simplest ingredients into extraordinary, exotic meals: bacalao, mofongo, black beans and rice—traditional Dominican dishes that she made all her own. Her cooking, her love, and her energy surrounded me; it was tangible and irresistible—a sweet, spicy, warm embrace of aromas and flavors.

I imagine every chef has their North Star, the one person who inspires them above all others. In my life, this someone is my Aunt Carmen. For her, the act of creating food was as important, if not more so, than eating it; it was her way of giving, of nurturing those she loved. Even though she died many years ago, every day when I step into the kitchen, she's with me, reminding me why I do what I do—because while food is sustenance, it's also love, beauty, and passion. Aunt Carmen's gift to me was the gift of knowledge; she enlightened me to the power that food has to connect us. Because of her, food is the way I share who I am, how I bring happiness to the world; by creating something delicious, something that makes you feel, and reminds you that you're alive.

Afternoons in Aunt Carmen's kitchen were defining times for me because they opened my eyes to the joy that cooking and food have to offer, to the warmth and vitality that a thoughtfully prepared meal can provide, to the sweetness of a life spent doing what you love—for those you love. All this was a far cry from what I was used to at home, where life was incredibly ordered and often tense. My father was very strict. Coming from a military family, his approach to our home life reflected this influence. I was firmly encouraged to listen to classical music. And I was taught to take my chores seriously or risk punishment. One of my chores was to help him cook on Saturdays in preparation for the big Sunday meal after church. For all his machismo, my father loves to cook.

# I imagine every chef has their North Star, the one person who inspires them above all others.

In our house, rice was served with everything—with bacalao, with my father's chickpea and tomato stew, even by itself, drizzled with homemade bay leaf–infused vinegar. There was never any shortage of rice at the table, which meant there was always an abundance of rice to be cleaned. Go figure; it was my job to clean the rice. We had a very long wooden bowl, shaped

like a shallow boat or canoe, and I would pour a heaping bag of rice into this bowl and then wash each grain individually, moving it from the larger pile at one end to the clean pile on the other. It was tedious and terrifying; if each grain wasn't sufficiently cleaned there'd be hell to pay. I can still remember the feel of that bowl on the tips of my fingers, the aged texture of the wood, and the smell of the starch on the rice as I ran each grain under the water.

Unlike at Aunt Carmen's house, these times in the kitchen weren't joyful and exhilarating; they were fraught with mixed emotions. I was frightened of doing a bad job, but I was also striving to live up to my father's expectations. In retrospect I know that those times were a way for us to bond, to create something together—but they were also a powerful lesson in never settling for anything less than your best. A hard lesson perhaps, but one that has become ingrained in my being.

The contrast of these two early experiences with food and cooking has shaped me—I would never be the chef I am today, let alone the person I am, if they hadn't happened. Life is full of different experiences, and to me they're like flavors. Sometimes the flavors don't seem like they meld well together, but once you give them the thought they deserve, when you find the right balance of this and that, then they come together to create something more complex and, ideally, something to be proud of. And sometimes, when life goes the way it should, the sweet experiences overwhelm the others just enough to make you stronger and more complete.

# Sweet Tomato Soup
## with Curried Whipped Cream

Serves: 4   Time: About 1 hour   Flavors: Sweet/Astringent/Spicy

People love this soup. I think it's because the first sip reminds you of childhood. With the second sip you notice the velvety consistency, how it sits on your tongue. Then you taste a complex blend of flavors just behind the sweet tomatoes—spicy ginger, luscious cream, a kick of curry—sophisticated yet somehow familiar is how my friend Jason describes it.

3 tablespoons grapeseed oil
1 tablespoon minced garlic
1 tablespoon grated ginger
1 cup diced onion
one 28-ounce can crushed Italian
   plum tomatoes

1 cup water
2 tablespoons gochujang paste
   (see Box, page 70)
1 tablespoon kosher salt
3 tablespoons sugar
½ cup heavy cream

1 Put the oil in a large saucepan over medium-high heat. When it glistens, add the garlic and ginger and sauté until just translucent, 1 to 2 minutes. Add the onion and continue cooking until soft and translucent as well, another 5 to 6 minutes.

2 Add the tomatoes, water, gochujang paste, salt, and sugar to the pan. Reduce the heat to medium-low and simmer for 25 minutes; remove from the heat.

3 Working in batches if necessary, purée the soup in a blender until it's velvety smooth (you can also use an immersion blender right in the pan). Add the cream and stir well to combine.

## Curried Whipped Cream

Curry Blend
4 cardamom pods
1 tablespoon coriander seeds
1 tablespoon cumin seeds
1 tablespoon ground turmeric
1 tablespoon white peppercorns
1½ teaspoons kosher salt

Curry Cream
1 cup heavy cream
1 tablespoon sugar
½ tablespoon Curry Blend
fresh cilantro leaves

1 In a dry sauté pan over medium heat, lightly toast the cardamom pods, coriander seeds, cumin seeds, and turmeric, starting with the largest spice first and gradually adding the others in order of decreasing size. Continue cooking, shaking the pan occasionally, until they're all aromatic, 3 to 4 minutes total. Let cool completely. Grind the toasted spices with the peppercorns and salt in a spice grinder until very fine. Keep in an airtight container for up to 3 months, or until ready to use.

2 In a large bowl, whip the cream until it holds soft peaks; add the sugar and curry blend. Whip again to blend completely. Serve a dollop of the curried cream on top of the soup and garnish with fresh cilantro leaves.

# Scallop and Banana Tartare
## with Jalapeño Vinaigrette

Serves: 4   Time: About 20 minutes   Flavors: Sweet/Spicy/Acidic

This is one of my favorite dishes. There's something so simple about it (no cooking, for one thing) but still so complex. The naturally sweet scallops and ripe banana combined with the spicy notes from the jalapeño vinaigrette are just . . . yummy.

Jalapeño Vinaigrette
1 jalapeño chile, seeded and chopped
3 tablespoons yuzu juice (see Box)
  or lemon juice
2 tablespoons sugar
3 tablespoons olive oil

½ pound bay scallops
1 green Thai chile, minced

1 tablespoon kosher salt
¼ cup olive oil
1 ripe banana
1 tablespoon sugar
freshly ground black pepper
fresh dill sprigs

**1** First make the Jalapeño Vinaigrette: Place the jalapeño, yuzu juice, sugar, and olive oil in a blender and blend until smooth; chill in the refrigerator until ready to use.

**2** Clean the bay scallops by removing the side muscle (abductor muscle) and rinsing them under cool water. Pat them dry with paper towels and cut them into ¼-inch dice. Put the scallops in a medium bowl and toss them with the Thai chile, 2 teaspoons of the salt, and 2 tablespoons of the olive oil; mix well.

**3** Peel the banana and cut it into ¼-inch dice. Put it in a small bowl and add the remaining teaspoon of salt, the remaining 2 tablespoons of olive oil, and the sugar. Mix gently to combine but try to retain the texture and shape of the banana.

**4** Put a spoonful of the banana mixture on each serving plate. Top with a generous spoonful of the scallops, a sprinkling of pepper, and a few dill sprigs. To serve, drizzle the vinaigrette around the bed of tartare.

Yuzu is a Japanese citrus fruit that is about the size of a tangerine and pretty sour. I love its fragrant, tangy flavor and use it a lot in my food. You don't see it everywhere, but one of my favorite stores in New York City is Kalustyan's—it's a spice and exotic ingredient paradise—and they always carry it (you can order it online; see page 15). In a pinch, swap lemon juice for the yuzu—it makes a perfectly good substitute.

# Chilled Ramen Noodles
## with Watermelon Tea

Serves: 4   Time: About 2 hours   Flavors: Sweet/Herbaceous/Astringent

In the Top Chef finals I served this with pork belly—for the vegetarian course. Oops. I guess I really was sick! In this version I skip the pork belly (like I should have then) and just go for a really beautiful chilled noodle soup. Making your own ramen noodles is just like making pasta—and like pasta, you want them to have a little tug to them, a bit of a bite. You also want to be sure to serve this dish really cold—sometimes in the summer I even freeze the tea to a slushy consistency for an awesome textural contrast.

2 cups all-purpose flour
1 teaspoon kosher salt
2 tablespoons Togarashi Salt
   (see page 53)
3 egg yolks
2 tablespoons water
olive oil
1 bunch scallions, sliced diagonally
fresh cilantro leaves

¼ cup smashed lemongrass (about
   1 stalk; see Box, page 31)
one 2-inch piece ginger, peeled and
   coarsely chopped
1 tablespoon kosher salt
3 tablespoons sugar
1 red Thai chile, minced
3 tablespoons lime juice
¼ cup water

Watermelon Tea
4 cups chopped seeded watermelon

**1** First make the Ramen Noodles: In a standing mixer fitted with the dough hook, combine the flour, salt, and Togarashi Salt and mix well. One at a time, add the egg yolks and mix, being sure to combine thoroughly after each addition. Add the water and continue to mix for 8 to 10 minutes, until the dough is quite tough. (If you're doing this by hand, you'll want to knead the dough on a well-floured surface for 10 to 20 minutes to get it to reach a tough, resistant consistency.)

**2** Remove the dough from the mixer, form it into a disk, wrap in plastic, and place in the fridge to chill for at least 30 minutes.

**3** Meanwhile, make the Watermelon Tea: Put all the ingredients in a blender and blend until smooth. Transfer to a large bowl, cover with plastic wrap, and let steep at room temperature for at least 30 minutes. Use a fine sieve to strain the tea and then put it in the fridge to chill for at least 1 hour (you want this tea to be ice cold!).

**4** Remove the dough from the fridge and cut it into quarters. If you're using a pasta maker, put the dough through the machine as you would for pasta until you get it as thin as possible, like you would for vermicelli. If you're doing this by hand, put the dough on a well-floured surface and using a rolling pin, roll each piece out until

it is no more than ⅛ inch thick. Make sure the dough is really floured so it doesn't stick together, and roll it up like a jellyroll (it should look like a long tube). Use a sharp knife to cut the roll into very thin vertical slices—about ⅛ inch wide—so when you unroll each slice you have a ramen noodle.

**5** Bring a large pot of well salted water to a boil. Add the ramen noodles and cook until just tender, about 2 minutes. Drain the noodles, put them in a large bowl, toss with a tablespoon or two of olive oil to prevent sticking, and chill in the fridge for 20 minutes.

**6** To serve, divide the chilled noodles among 4 individual soup bowls, pour the ice-cold watermelon tea over them, and garnish with the scallions and cilantro.

# Grilled Duck Breast
## with Honey-Pepper Glaze

Serves: 4   Time: About 30 minutes   Flavors: Sweet/Salty/Herbaceous

I'm usually all about fresh herbs and spices, but thyme and oregano are two exceptions—when dried, their volatile oils become really potent and intense, which I love. Here I use dried thyme (which you find in many Middle Eastern dishes) in the glaze and seriously, the concentration of the herb's oils paired with the grilled duck is simply awesome. No doubt this is a rustic dish, but it tastes fancy—it's perfect for a special occasion or a weekend barbecue.

Honey-Pepper Glaze
1 cup Italian or other good-quality
  honey
1 teaspoon kosher salt
2 tablespoons dried thyme
1 tablespoon freshly ground
  black pepper

4 small Peking or Muscovy duck
  breasts (see Box)
kosher salt
freshly ground black pepper

**1** First make the Honey-Pepper Glaze: In a small saucepan over medium-low heat, warm the honey. Add the salt, thyme, and pepper and stir to combine. Remove from the heat and set aside.

**2** Preheat a grill or grill pan to medium heat. Pat the duck breasts dry with paper towels and season the flesh side well with salt and pepper.

**3** Place the duck fat side down on the grill and cook for about 8 minutes, until the fat has completely rendered. Flip the breasts and cook for another 2 to 4 minutes.

**4** Transfer the breasts to a cutting board and brush with the Honey-Pepper Glaze on both sides so they're completely lacquered (put the remaining glaze in a serving dish for additional drizzling at the table). Let the duck rest for a few minutes before cutting, then slice it into thick portions on the diagonal. Place the sliced duck on a platter and serve family style with the remaining glaze on the side.

Muscovy and Peking duck need to be handled slightly differently based on their fat content. If you're using Muscovy duck breasts here, you may want to salt the fat side of the breasts and let them sit for 20 to 30 minutes to remove some of the moisture and help ensure a crisp skin. If you're using Peking, you don't have to bother.

# Saigon Burgers
# with Ginger Glaze and Thai Basil Mayo

Serves: 4    Time: About 45 minutes    Flavors: Sweet/Herbaceous/Astringent

Burgers have become my new fetish—I'm sort of obsessed. For me, it's all about the burger blend, which is why in my recipe I've increased the fat content by adding brisket to give the meat a special lusciousness. Then, as opposed to adding ketchup at the end, I brush the burgers with a sweet, tangy Vietnamese-style glaze throughout the cooking process so the meat is actually infused with flavor.

Ginger Glaze
¼ cup chopped ginger
2 tablespoons chopped garlic
2 tablespoons sugar
½ cup light soy sauce
2 tablespoons toasted sesame oil

Thai Basil Mayo
2 cups Thai basil leaves
1 cup mayonnaise
1 teaspoon kosher salt
1 ice cube

1 pound beef, preferably chuck
  or sirloin
¼ pound brisket
2 tablespoons kosher salt
4 sesame brioche buns or other rolls
1 cup shredded iceberg lettuce
½ red onion, thinly sliced
fresh Thai basil leaves
fresh cilantro leaves
fresh mint leaves
Sriracha sauce

1 First make the Ginger Glaze: Combine the ginger, garlic, sugar, soy sauce, and sesame oil in a blender and blend until smooth; set aside.

2 Then make the mayo: Put a medium saucepan of well salted water over medium-high heat. While the water comes to a boil, set up a bowl of ice water next to the stove. When the water reaches a boil, add the Thai basil leaves and blanch for 20 seconds to set the color and let them wilt. Drain the Thai basil and immediately plunge into the ice water to stop the cooking process. Remove the leaves and squeeze them dry. Put the Thai basil leaves in a blender with the mayonnaise, salt, and ice cube and blend until smooth.

3 Preheat a grill or grill pan over high heat. Cut both meats into cubes and place in a food processor with the salt. Pulse until ground—you want the meat to be chopped but you don't want it to lose its texture or get tough. Form into 4 patties, make them firm so they don't fall apart during cooking.

4 Brush the patties on both sides with the glaze. Place over the hottest part of the grill and cook until they release easily from the grill, then turn over, brush with more glaze, and continuing cooking. Cooking time will be about 3 minutes per side for very rare and another minute per side for each increasing stage of doneness. When the burgers are done, brush them again with the glaze.

5 Meanwhile, toast the buns and place each bun open on a plate. Spread the Thai Basil Mayo on both sides of the buns. Then place ¼ cup shredded lettuce, a few slices of red onion, and a few leaves of Thai basil, cilantro, and mint on the bottom of each bun. Place the grilled burgers on top of the garnishes, drizzle with Sriracha sauce, and top with the other half of the bun to serve.

# Braised Short Ribs
# with Lemongrass Honey

**Serves: 4   Time: About 4 hours   Flavors: Sweet/Salty/Herbaceous**

I add pineapple to many of my braises for two reasons: First it offers up a fabulous flavor; in this recipe the sweet, tangy taste combined with the lemongrass and honey is totally exotic and unexpected. But I also love using pineapple because it contains an enzyme called bromelain. Not to get too technical, but bromelain breaks down the fiber structure of the protein in the beef—helping make these ribs super-tender as well as fabulously flavorful.

**5 pounds boneless beef short ribs**
**2 tablespoons kosher salt**
**2 tablespoons grapeseed oil**
**one 2-inch piece ginger, cut in half**
**¼ cup smashed lemongrass (about**
**  1 stalk)**
**2 cups roughly chopped pineapple**
**  (no need to peel)**

**1 cup soy sauce**
**1 gallon good-quality chicken stock**

Lemongrass Honey
**2 cups smashed lemongrass**
**  (6 to 8 stalks)**
**1 tablespoon kosher salt**
**2 cups Italian or other good-quality**
**  honey**

**1** Preheat the oven to 300°F.

**2** Pat the ribs dry with paper towels and season them well with the salt. Add the oil to a large, deep pot set over high heat. When the oil shimmers, sear the ribs on all sides until well browned, 12 to 15 minutes. Work in batches if necessary to make sure the ribs brown and don't steam. Set the ribs aside after searing them.

**3** Meanwhile, place the ginger in a small sauté pan set over medium-high heat and char it on all sides (this will bring a deeper, more complex flavor to the broth).

**4** In the pot used to cook the ribs, combine the smashed lemongrass, pineapple, soy sauce, chicken stock, and charred ginger over low heat. Bring the mixture to a simmer and add the reserved ribs to the pan; cover with a lid or foil. Transfer the ribs to the oven and braise for 2½ to 3 hours, until fork tender.

**5** Meanwhile, make the Lemongrass Honey: Finely chop the smashed lemongrass. Combine it with the salt and honey in a medium saucepan set over medium heat. When the mixture begins to simmer, reduce the heat to low and cook for 10 more minutes. Remove from the heat.

**6** Put the lemongrass mixture in a blender and blend until smooth, then refrigerate until ready to use. (I would eat it finely blended without straining, but if you prefer, press the mixture through a fine sieve to remove any remaining fibers.)

**7** When the ribs are done, remove them from the liquid and set aside. Strain the braising liquid through a fine sieve and add it back to the pan. Reduce over medium-high heat, stirring frequently, until it is the consistency of light cream and just coats the back of a spoon. Return the ribs to the pan and toss to coat.

**8** Turn the oven to broil. Transfer the ribs to a sheet pan, brush each one with the glaze, and broil for 2 to 3 minutes to lacquer the exterior, keeping an eye on them to make sure they don't burn. Serve immediately.

To release all the fabulous aromatic flavor in lemongrass, I smash the stalks before chopping them. Just set the side of a large knife down on the stalk and press down really hard—the stalk should burst a bit and flatten.

# Slow-Cooked
# Asian Pork Belly

**Serves: 2 to 4   Time: About 2 hours   Flavors: Sweet/Salty/Nutty**

This beautifully succulent, fatty, barbecued pork is super-rich and super-easy—it's also a great example of a sweet, salty, nutty flavor combo that you're probably used to tasting in restaurants but not used to dishing up at home. I love this pork with sambal—a spicy chile paste—to perfectly balance out the sweetness factor. Serve this with rice, pickles, and maybe a fresh herb salad.

1 pound pork belly
3 cups water
1 cup light soy sauce
¼ cup sesame oil

1½ cups sugar
¼ cup plus 2 tablespoons hoisin sauce
fresh cilantro leaves
toasted sesame seeds

**1** Heat a grill or put a large sauté pan over high heat. Put the pork belly on the grill or sauté pan, skin side down, and cook until charred, or cook over high heat until the skin is golden brown. Transfer to a plate and set aside.

**2** Preheat the oven to 350°F.

**3** In a large ovenproof saucepan with a lid, combine the water, soy sauce, sesame oil, sugar, and hoisin sauce. Place over medium-high heat and bring to a simmer.

**4** Add the pork belly to the pan, cover, and cook in the oven for about 1½ hours, until the pork is fork-tender. Check the pork every 30 minutes or so; if the liquid level seems low, add water as needed. When the pork is done, remove the lid and continue cooking until a glaze forms over the pork and the skin turns a deep, dark, Madeira color.

**5** Transfer the pork to a cutting board and let cool. Meanwhile, carefully strain the liquid into a medium saucepan over medium-high heat. Reduce until syrupy.

**6** To serve, thinly slice the pork belly, drizzle with the glaze, and sprinkle with the cilantro and sesame seeds.

# Roasted Butternut Squash
# with Spiced Caramel

**Serves: 4 to 6   Time: About 1 hour   Flavors: Sweet/Earthy/Bitter**

When I was young, Thanksgiving was my favorite holiday. My cousins from Michigan would drive thirteen hours to Connecticut for a big family football game and a huge meal. After hours of playing in the cold, I always looked forward to the butternut squash the most. This is my updated version of our family's classic—same sweet squash, but with the addition of some beautiful warm fall spices and a sweet kick of caramel.

**2 butternut squashes**
**2 teaspoons kosher salt**
**1 teaspoon red pepper flakes**
**¼ cup olive oil**

**Spiced Caramel**
**4 cloves**

**3 allspice berries**
**½ teaspoon kosher salt**
**½ cup packed brown sugar**
**½ cup heavy cream**
**2 tablespoons unsalted butter**

**1** Preheat the oven to 350°F.

**2** Cut the squash in half and use a spoon to remove all the seeds, scrape the flesh of any remaining strings, and discard. Season the insides of the squash with the salt and red pepper flakes and drizzle with the oil. Place the squash halves flesh side down in a roasting pan or on a sheet pan and cook for 30 to 45 minutes, until tender when pierced with a fork.

**3** Meanwhile, lightly toast the cloves and allspice in a small dry sauté pan over medium-low heat until the essential oils are released, about 2 minutes. Let cool completely and grind with the salt in a spice grinder until fine.

**4** Put the brown sugar in a small saucepan over medium heat. Stirring frequently, allow the sugar to caramelize. When the sugar just begins to turn amber, add the ground spices and mix to combine. Immediately add the cream—it will bubble up, so be careful—followed by the butter; cook for 3 to 4 more minutes, until it reaches a sauce-like consistency. Set aside and, if necessary, warm over low heat just before serving.

**5** When the squash is done, spoon out large chunks and put them in serving bowls. Drizzle the sauce over the squash and serve.

# Grilled Corn with
## Sweet Coconut Flakes and Spicy Mayo

**Serves: 4   Time: About 30 minutes   Flavors: Sweet/Spicy/Smoky**

Growing up in Durham, CT we lived on the top of a hill right next to a cornfield that seemed to go on forever—as far as I could see there were corn stalks stretching out into the distance. This dish reminds me of that endless field as the sweetness lingers on your tongue and the smokiness of the chipotle hints at corn blistering on the grill. Imagine the corn you buy on the streets of Mexico jazzed up with some Southeast Asian spice. That's what this recipe is and, man, is it good. I happen to be naturally drawn to the flavor of char, so I like to grill the corn until it's black in spots. I swear that smoky aroma is intoxicating; if I could, I'd bottle it.

**4 ears corn, shucked**
**4 tablespoons (½ stick)**
**unsalted butter**
**2 fresh thyme sprigs**
**¼ cup sweetened coconut flakes,**
  **lightly toasted**

Spicy Mayo
**2 cups mayonnaise**
**¼ cup Sriracha sauce**
**1 tablespoon kosher salt**

**1** Preheat a grill to medium-high.

**2** Put a large pot of water over medium-high heat. Add the corn, butter, and thyme and bring to a boil, then reduce to a simmer. Continue cooking until the corn is tender, about 10 minutes. Remove from the heat and drain; set the corn aside until you're ready to grill.

**3** While the corn cooks, make the Spicy Mayo: Combine the mayonnaise, Sriracha sauce, and salt in a blender and blend until smooth; set aside.

**4** Grill the corn, turning occasionally, until nicely charred on all sides. To serve, spoon a dollop or more of the Spicy Mayo on each ear of corn and garnish with the coconut flakes.

# Shaved Ice with Green Tea Syrup
# and Fruity Pebbles

Serves: 4    Time: About 30 minutes    Flavors: Sweet/Spicy/Smoky

Shaved ice is huge in Asia, and on a hot summer day there's nothing like it. I infuse this ice with green tea syrup for an exotic flavor boost. And yes, you read the recipe title right: Then I grab Fruity Pebbles cereal to sprinkle it on top. Those sweet, crunchy little bites dazzle up this dessert perfectly. Add some fresh fruit, sit back, and chill out.

½ cup sugar
½ cup water
½ teaspoon kosher salt
½ cup green tea
4 cups ice

Fruity Pebbles cereal
fresh fruit such as strawberries, kiwi, or pineapple, cut into small pieces (optional)

1 In a medium saucepan over medium-high heat, bring the sugar, water, and salt to a boil, then reduce the heat to a simmer. Add the green tea, allow the mixture to return to a simmer, then transfer to a bowl or pitcher and refrigerate until very cold.

2 Working in batches, put the ice in a blender or food processor and grind into fine pieces. Fill a cup or small soup bowl with ground ice and pour the green tea syrup over the top. Garnish with Fruity Pebbles and any fresh fruit you like.

# Vanilla Bean and Cardamom
## Tapioca Pudding

**Serves: 4   Time:  About 1 hour with chilling   Flavors: Sweet/Earthy/Salty**

Sweet, creamy, sexy. Trust me: This isn't the tapioca you grew up with.
I infuse this retro pudding with the essence of coconut and the exotic
flavors of vanilla, cardamom, and star anise for a totally modern take.
If you want to keep it classic, top each dish with whipped cream. Personally,
I'd crank up the spice factor with a dollop of cardamom whipped cream—
simply add a teaspoon or so of ground cardamom to the cream.

1 cup large pearl tapioca
4 cups whole milk or soy milk
1 cup coconut water
½ cup sugar
1 vanilla bean, split

6 cardamom pods
1 star anise
½ teaspoon kosher salt
whipped cream (optional)

**1** Rinse and soak the tapioca in water for 20 minutes to remove the exterior starch.

**2** Meanwhile, put the milk, coconut water, sugar, vanilla bean, cardamom pods,
star anise, and salt in large saucepan and bring to a simmer over medium-high
heat. Reduce the heat and cook low and slow for 20 minutes.

**3** Use a slotted spoon to fish out the spices and discard them. Drain the tapioca
and add it to the milk mixture. Continue to cook at a low simmer until the pearls
are clear, 15 to 20 minutes. Transfer to a bowl and chill in the refrigerator for at
least 20 minutes.

**4** Spoon the pudding into 4 individual serving dishes, top with whipped cream,
if desired, and serve.

# Chocolate Brownie
## with Gula Melaka Toffee and Chai Milkshake

Serves: 6 to 8    Time: 2 hours    Flavors: Sweet/Nutty/Earthy

Gula melaka is Malaysian palm sugar. It's very similar to brown sugar in that it has a deep, molasses-like flavor, giving this toffee a rich earthiness that I think is more interesting than traditional toffee. The toffee is amazing, the brownies are awesome, but in some ways I think it's the chai milkshake that really brings it all together. My close friend Ricky, who loves his morning cereal, always says that a milkshake reminds him of the those last few delicious sips of milk he gets at the bottom of the bowl.

1 cup (2 sticks) unsalted butter
grapeseed oil for greasing
1 cup sugar
2 cups all-purpose flour
½ cup unsweetened cocoa
  powder
1½ teaspoons kosher salt
1 teaspoon baking powder
3 large eggs

Toffee
2 cups sugar
¼ cup gula melaka
  (palm sugar)
½ teaspoon kosher salt
1 cup heavy cream
4 tablespoons (½ stick) unsalted
  butter, cut into small pieces

**1** Melt the butter in a small saucepan over medium heat and set aside.

**2** Preheat the oven to 350°F and lightly grease an 8-inch baking dish with oil. In a large bowl, combine the sugar, flour, cocoa powder, salt, and baking powder. Add the eggs one at time, integrating each thoroughly before adding the next. Add the butter and mix until smooth.

**3** Pour the batter into the prepared baking dish and bake for 25 minutes, or until a toothpick inserted in the center comes out clean. Cool to room temperature and then cut to desired sizes.

**4** While the brownies bake, make the Toffee: Combine the sugar, gula melaka, and salt in a medium saucepan over medium heat. Cook, stirring frequently, until the sugar melts, begins to caramelize, and turns amber. Add the cream—it will bubble up profusely—and once the bubbles dissipate, begin adding the butter one piece at a time. Once all the butter has been added, cook over medium-low heat for 2 minutes, or until it reaches the consistency of thick cream (and coats the back of a dipped spoon). Remove from the heat.

**5** Serve the toffee drizzled over the brownies along with a glass of the chai milkshake on the side.

# Chai Milkshake

1 cup basmati rice
4 cardamom pods
2 star anise

¼ cup sugar
3 cups whole milk
½ cup ice

**1** In a medium saucepan with a lid, lightly toast the basmati rice over medium heat, shaking the pan occasionally, until the grains become aromatic and just begin to color. Add the cardamom pods and star anise and continue cooking, shaking the pan frequently to avoid burning the rice.

**2** Add the sugar and milk to the pan and bring to a simmer; remove from the heat. Cover the pan and let the rice mixture steep for 10 minutes to fully release all the flavors and give them time to meld. Use a fine sieve to strain the mixture into a large bowl, removing both the rice and the spices; put the bowl in the fridge to chill for about 15 minutes.

**3** When fully chilled, put the mixture in a blender and blend with the ice until smooth. Keep refrigerated until ready to serve.

# Turmeric-Onion Jam

Serves: 6 to 8    Time: About 30 minutes    Flavors: Sweet/Astringent/Spicy

An Asian alternative to jelly, in the restaurant I serve it as a condiment for fish and chicken, but at home I use it to jazz up my late-night sandwiches: my killer combo of peanut butter, onion jam, and kimchi is a little taste of Korea without the air miles.

3 tablespoons grapeseed oil
1 tablespoon mustard seeds
2 tablespoons ground turmeric
2 cups sliced onions
3 tablespoons minced garlic

3 tablespoons minced ginger
½ cup sugar
¼ cup seasoned rice wine
   vinegar
2 tablespoons kosher salt

**1** Put a medium sauté pan over low heat and add the oil. When it's hot, add the mustard seeds and toast lightly for 30 seconds to 1 minute, until they pop.

**2** Add the turmeric, onions, garlic, and ginger and stir to combine. Sweat over low heat until the onions are translucent but not coloring, 6 to 8 minutes.

**3** Add the sugar to the pan and cook until the onions thicken and begin to shine, another 8 to 10 minutes. Add the vinegar and cook for another 5 minutes, or until the acidity subsides and the liquid has reduced to a glaze. Season with the salt, cool, and serve as desired or store in an airtight container in the fridge for up to 2 weeks.

# Candied Ginger
# and Juniper Breadcrumbs

Serves: 4 to 6    Time: About 20 minutes    Flavors: Sweet/Spicy/Floral

Juniper is a flavor you're probably familiar with if you drink gin—it's floral and works beautifully with the sweetness of candied ginger. This recipe is great served with lamb, venison, beef, and even fish. It's also my go-to topping for gratins, a great mix-in for salads instead of croutons, and if you want a quick, no-work dinner, toss with some pasta and you're all set. Personally, I use and abuse this stuff!

½ cup (1 stick) unsalted butter
½ cup grapeseed oil
2 cups panko (Japanese breadcrumbs)
1 teaspoon kosher salt
10 juniper berries, crushed and
   coarsely chopped

¼ cup candied ginger, cut into
   small dice
1 tablespoon black peppercorns,
   crushed
2 tablespoons fleur de sel or other
   high quality salt

**1** Combine the butter and grapeseed oil in a medium sauté pan over medium-high heat. When the butter melts and the oil is hot, reduce the heat to medium, add the panko and salt and cook, stirring frequently, until golden brown, 6 to 8 minutes. Using a slotted spoon, transfer the breadcrumbs to a plate, draining any excess butter-oil mixture (if there's any remaining fat you can save it for another use).

**2** In a medium bowl, combine the juniper berries, ginger, peppercorns, and fleur de sel and mix well. Add the breadcrumbs to the bowl, toss to combine, and use as desired or store in an airtight container for up to 2 days.

# Curried White
## Chocolate Sauce

**Serves: 6 to 8    Time: About 15 minutes    Flavors: Sweet/Spicy/Astringent**

Don't freak out. Curry and white chocolate are a great combination—just one that
you've probably never thought of putting together before. The truth is that the
deep aromatic spice of the curry and the sweetness of the white chocolate are made
for each other. I love this sauce drizzled over salmon, or, if you want to take it up
a notch at a party, dip barbecue-flavored potato chips in this sauce and spoon a
dollop of caviar on top.

Curry Powder
**4 cardamom pods**
**one 2-inch piece cinnamon**
**4 cloves**
**2 teaspoons coriander seeds**
**2 teaspoons cumin seeds**

**1 tablespoon ground turmeric**
**1 teaspoon kosher salt**

**1 cup white chocolate chips**
**3 cups heavy cream**
**1 teaspoon kosher salt**

**1** First make the Curry Powder: In a dry sauté pan over medium heat, lightly
toast the cardamom pods, cinnamon, coriander seeds, cumin seeds, and turmeric,
starting with the largest spice first and gradually adding in order of decreasing
size. Continue cooking, shaking the pan occasionally, until they're aromatic,
3 to 4 minutes total. Let cool completely. Grind the spices, including the salt,
in a spice grinder until very fine.

**2** In a double boiler set over medium heat, melt the white chocolate and stir until
smooth. Add the cream, salt, and 3 tablespoons Curry Powder and continue cooking
until everything is well blended and the mixture is smooth. Remove from the heat
and serve, or put in an airtight container and refrigerate for up to 2 weeks. Reheat
before using.

Cured Watermelon Crudo with Thyme

## Goat Cheese Fondue

Tostones in Garlic Oil with Bay Leaf Salt

## Spiced Onion Rings with Togarashi Salt

Sunny-Side Up Egg with Chinese Sausage and "Takeout" Fried Rice

## General Tso's Sweetbreads

Fried Maple-Glazed Bacon

## Ramen with Spam Broth

Flaked Cod Fish Bacalao with Green Olive and Tomato Stew

## Slow-Cooked "Canned" Tuna

## Salted Pine Nut Toffee

Sake and Cheddar Cheese Sauce

# Salty 2

# Salty | What Doesn't Kill You . . .

**Like the flavors and textures that come together** to make up a perfect dish, life is a lesson in contrasts. When I was on Top Chef, I experienced such a vast range of emotions, such conflicting feelings, that it's difficult to put them into words. For those who watched the show, you saw me elated with pride at times, but also racked by illness and overcome by gratitude. It was a crazy time, but it made me a stronger person—and more important, a better one.

After we completed the semifinals and were headed to the judges' table to see who would progress to the finals to become Top Chef, I became very ill. To this day I vividly remember being in the van with my fellow contestants, driving down the highway in Singapore, feeling completely fine, and then suddenly being hit, like a giant ocean wave that catches you unaware, by an overwhelming sense that I was going to be sick. I begged the driver to pull over, and within minutes, maybe seconds, I was ill on the side of the road. I vaguely remember thinking this can't be happening, and then the thought flashed through my mind that everyone in the van was probably thinking, yeah, this is good, this is perfect, he's out.

When we finally got to the judges' table and Padma announced that all contestants had to approach the table, I still was not feeling well. I kept trying to focus and tell myself to dig deep, I'd come so far. When the moment for the final verdict came, part of me truly just wanted to go home, to be with my mother, to be done with it all. But the other part of me knew I'd sacrificed so much to get here and that this was a journey I was meant to complete. When they finally announced that it was Kelly who was going home, not me, I broke down and started crying— part of me thought it would be me going home, part of me wished it was.

As the remaining finalists, our next assignment was to create the meal of our lives, and we were each assigned a sous chef to help us. Thankfully I got Hung, who knew both my style of food and Asian cooking. Everyone else spent that night working on their menus and their shopping lists, but I knew I had to get rest or I would never be able to compete, so I went to bed knowing I'd wake up and this would all be over, that I'd feel like myself again.

Instead when I woke up the next morning I was no better. My body was sore, and I had a bad headache. After seeing two doctors, they said there was an injection they could give me that was my only chance to stay in the competition. My heart leapt and I took that chance. The producers allowed me to use a cell phone to talk to Hung so he could shop for me, and while I didn't have the capacity to plan a meal, I gave him general instructions on what I needed to prep and cook and he made sure we were ready. When the time came, I showered and shaved, I wore gloves and a mask to protect the other chefs and the diners, and I just kept thinking: This is no longer about you, this is about your son, your mother, your Aunt Carmen, your father, all the great chefs who have taught you, the fans who support you, the producers who believe in you. I also remembered what my Little League coach used to say before each game: "Who's gonna step up and be the star?" Back then I always said to myself, I am, I'm going to light this up. And that's what I did.

For that competition I made an insane menu: It started with homemade ramen noodles served with pork belly char siu and watermelon tea. For the second course I did an Asian-style bouillabaisse over sautéed rouget and poached cuttlefish. Then I kicked it into high gear with this awesome sautéed duck foie gras with marshmallow and a chilled cherry shooter. Even though I was sick, I felt like I was on fire with this menu, but as I was putting it out for the judges I heard them call for the vegetarian course and in my head I just went, "Okay Angelo, for a vegetarian course you're serving pork belly."

At this point, when we all went up to the judges' table to see who had won, I wasn't expecting to win Top Chef anymore (come on, I had served pork for a vegetarian course!). I had already done what I set out to do. When I got to the stove, when I cooked that meal, I knew I had won what I had come to win for myself: I had truly given everything I had—more than I even knew I had. When they announced that Kevin was Top Chef, I was honored to be there with him. Every emotion that I had tasted on this journey was now part of me: joy, sadness, pride, humility, and especially gratitude. Yes, I had shed some tears (okay, a lot) on this journey, you could even say I had tasted more than my fair share of salt, but I could go home happy.

# Cured Watermelon Crudo with Thyme

Serves: 4   Time: 45 minutes   Flavors: Salty/Sweet Herbaceous

This is one of my favorite ways to start or finish a summer meal—it's tantalizing enough to get your taste buds going and refreshing enough to cleanse your palate. The key here is to retain the shape of the melon once it's cut; you want it to look cubed and pristine, almost like tuna sashimi.

2 cups seeded cubed watermelon (1-inch cubes)
2 teaspoons kosher salt
1 tablespoon fresh thyme leaves

3 tablespoons olive oil
¼ teaspoon freshly ground black pepper

**1** Put the watermelon on a sheet pan and sprinkle it with the salt. Place it in the fridge to chill for 30 minutes.

**2** Remove the watermelon from the fridge, add the thyme, olive oil, and pepper and toss very gently to combine. Serve immediately.

# Goat Cheese Fondue

Serves: 4   Time: About 20 minutes   Flavors: Salty/Herbaceous/Earthy

Growing up, my sister Lisa always had fondue on her birthday—it was a family tradition. It was also traditional for all seven of us kids to fight to get our skewers into the pot at the same time. Inevitably a few pieces of the bread would end up in the bottom, and then we'd compete to see who could fish those out. I have great memories of those meals, so I wanted to create a dish that reminded me of them. After spending time in Provence, in the south of France, I fell in love with goat cheese and decided to tweak my mom's fondue recipe by altering the main ingredient. The goat cheese adds a slightly sophisticated spin to this childhood favorite.

1 tablespoon unsalted butter
3 tablespoons diced shallots
2 fresh thyme sprigs
¼ cup dry white wine
1 tablespoon sugar
1 cup heavy cream

2 cups soft goat cheese
½ teaspoon kosher salt
¼ teaspoon freshly ground
   white pepper
endive leaves or toasted baguette
   for dipping

**1** Melt the butter in a medium saucepan over medium heat. Reduce the heat to low, add the shallots and thyme, and sweat for 3 to 5 minutes, until the shallots are completely soft.

**2** Increase the heat to medium and add the wine and sugar. Continue cooking, stirring occasionally, until the wine is reduced by half, another 2 to 3 minutes. Remove the thyme sprigs and discard. Add the heavy cream and reduce by half again.

**3** Reduce the heat to low and gradually add the goat cheese, about ¼ cup at a time. Be sure to moderate the heat so the mixture does not become grainy. Using a whisk or wooden spoon, continue stirring until all the cheese is thoroughly combined. Add the salt and white pepper and mix well. Transfer to a deep dish and serve immediately with endive leaves or toasted baguette for dipping.

# Tostones in Garlic Oil
# with Bay Leaf Salt

Serves: 4   Time: About 30 minutes   Flavors: Salty/Floral/Astringent

Just writing this recipe takes me back home. This is a dish I mastered with the help of my Aunt Carmen. It's a signature for our family and one that very distinctly represents my Dominican side—where I really found my true passion and love for spices. In Dominican cooking bay leaf and garlic are ever present and very subtly used as foundational flavors. Just thinking about this recipe makes me feel the weight of the pan in my hand as I smash the plantains and I can almost smell the wonderful aroma of the garlic oil. Wow—maybe I'll make this tonight.

6 dried bay leaves
2 tablespoons kosher salt
grapeseed oil

2 plantains (green bananas), peeled
  and cut into 1-inch-thick disks
2 tablespoons minced garlic
Tabasco sauce

1 Combine the bay leaves and salt in a spice grinder and grind until fine. Set aside.

2 Pour enough oil into a large pot to come about 3 inches up the sides. Turn the heat to high and bring to 325°F, as measured by a deep-fry or candy thermometer. Meanwhile, line a sheet pan with paper towels and put it by the stove to hold the tostones as they come out of the oil.

3 When the oil is hot, add the plantain slices to the pan and cook until they are golden on each side, about 3 minutes total. Using a slotted spoon, transfer to the prepared sheet pan to drain.

4 Use a heavy pot to smash the plantains until slightly flattened and add them back to the hot oil. Cook until crisp and lightly browned, another 3 minutes. Transfer to the sheet pan and immediately sprinkle with the bay leaf salt.

5 In a small skillet, heat 3 tablespoons of oil over medium-high heat. Add the garlic and cook for about 1 minute, until just aromatic.

6 Place the tostones on a serving dish, drizzle with the garlic oil, add a few shakes of Tabasco sauce, and serve immediately.

# Spiced Onion Rings
## with Togarashi Salt

Serves: 4 to 6    Time: About 30 minutes    Flavors: Salty/Sweet/Spicy

These onion rings have a light, crisp exterior with a sweet, tender interior—just like a great onion ring should. But here's the thing—these are jacked up with a spicy Japanese salt blend. They have a touch of heat, a bit of bite, and just a hint of the sea to them, thanks to the nori. It's an amazing flavor combination that you can use to spice up much more than onion rings—think scrambled eggs, fish, chicken, anything that cries out for a boost of flavor from the Far East.

Togarashi Salt
2 tablespoons black sesame seeds
¼ cup red pepper flakes
1 tablespoon dried orange peel
   (see Box)
3 sheets nori seaweed
½ teaspoon ground ginger
1 tablespoon sansho or Szechuan
   peppercorns
¾ cup kosher salt

1 cup all-purpose flour
1½ teaspoons kosher salt
1 cup water
grapeseed oil
2 large onions, cut into ½-inch discs
   and separated

**1** First make the Togarashi Salt: In a small dry sauté pan over medium heat, lightly toast the sesame seeds, 2 to 3 minutes. Remove from the heat and let cool.

**2** Put the sesame seeds, red pepper flakes, orange peel, seaweed, ginger, and peppercorns in a spice grinder and blend until fine. Mix the spices with the kosher salt in a small bowl and set aside.

**3** In a large bowl, mix together the flour, salt, and water; stir until smooth.

**4** Pour enough oil into a large pot to come about 3 inches up the sides. Turn the heat to high and bring to 325°F, as measured by a deep-fry or candy thermometer. Meanwhile, line a sheet pan with paper towels and put it by the stove to hold the onion rings as they come out of the oil.

**5** When the oil is ready, dip each onion ring in the batter. Working in batches so you don't overcrowd the pot, add the battered onions to the pot. When the onion rings are golden and crisp, 5 to 7 minutes, use a slotted spoon to carefully transfer them to the prepared sheet pan to drain any excess oil. While they're still hot, sprinkle the onion rings generously with the togarashi salt and serve.

To make dried orange peel, use a zester to remove just the outer layer of skin from an orange. Leave the peel in a warm place to dry out for 30 minutes to 1 hour. If you're in a hurry, put the peel in a microwave, zapping it on high at 15-second intervals until dry.

# Sunny-Side Up Egg with Chinese Sausage and "Takeout" Fried Rice

Serves: 2   Time: About 20 minutes   Flavors: Salty/Smoky/Umami

Full disclosure: I love takeout. Chinese, Thai, Vietnamese, Japanese, you name it. I live in New York, I work long, crazy hours, and sometimes there's nothing better than dialing a number and having dinner brought to my door—except maybe freezing the leftover rice and using it on my day off to whip up this amazing dish. I promise, once you taste this you'll never throw out your leftover takeout rice again. This recipe is insanely simple, and it's a cool way to add some Asian flavor to your morning (afternoon or evening) meal.

| | |
|---|---|
| 2 large eggs | 2 tablespoons grated ginger |
| pinch of kosher salt | 2 cups leftover rice |
| ½ cup minced Chinese sausage, chorizo, or other breakfast sausage | ¼ cup light soy sauce |
| | 1 tablespoon sesame oil |
| 3 tablespoons grapeseed oil | 3 tablespoons finely chopped scallions |
| 2 tablespoons minced garlic | |

**1** Put a small nonstick sauté pan over medium heat. When it's hot, crack 1 egg into the pan and cook it sunny-side up until the white begins to set. Lightly salt the white of the egg, then add the sausage to the white and continue cooking until just set.

**2** Meanwhile, put a wok or large sauté pan over high heat. When the pan is really hot, add the oil along with the garlic and ginger, and cook for about 1 minute, until aromatic.

**3** Crack the remaining egg into the wok and using a wooden spoon, scramble it quickly. Add the rice, stirring to separate it, and continue cooking and stirring the mixture for another 5 minutes. Season with the soy sauce; to retain its nutty flavor, drizzle the sesame oil on the rice at the very end of cooking. Transfer the rice to a serving plate or bowl, sprinkle the scallions over the rice, and place the fried egg on top. To serve, cut up the fried egg or slice it in wedges like a pizza, spoon the rice into bowls, and top each with some of the fried egg.

A hot wok gives food a unique flavor; think of the way a grill gives food a special kind of taste. The flavor a wok provides is called the "wok hay," and it comes from the "dragon's breath," the really high flame that heats the pan. You won't get this same flavor with a regular pan, but this dish will still rock—even if you don't have a wok!

# General Tso's
## Sweetbreads

Serves: 4    Time: About 1½ hours plus overnight soaking of the sweetbreads
Flavors:  Salty/Sweet/Floral

As I mentioned in my last recipe, I'm pro-delivery. When I get home late at night I love to order in General Tso's chicken and have it delivered to my door. This is my take on that amazing dish—the only catch being you have to actually make it yourself.

1 pound sweetbreads
2 cups whole milk
2 cups water
1 cup all-purpose flour
grapeseed oil

Cassia Breadcrumbs
½ cup (1 stick) unsalted butter
1½ cups grapeseed oil
2 cups breadcrumbs
one 4-inch piece cassia or cinnamon,
   ground

3 tablespoons Togarashi Salt (page 53)
3 tablespoons orange zest

General Tso's Sauce
¼ cup soy sauce
2 tablespoons calamansi juice (see Box)
   or lemon juice
2 tablespoons gochujang paste (see
   Box, page 70)
¼ cup sugar
1 tablespoon sesame oil

**1** Put the sweetbreads, milk, and water in a dish and be sure the sweetbreads are fully submerged in the liquid; add more water if needed to fully submerge. Soak the sweetbreads overnight to remove any bitterness.

**2** Make the Cassia Breadcrumbs: Put the butter and oil in a large, deep pan over medium-high heat. When the butter has melted and the oil is hot, add the breadcrumbs and cook, stirring frequently, until they turn golden brown. Meanwhile, prepare a sheet pan lined with paper towels and place it next to the stove. As soon as the breadcrumbs begin to brown, transfer them with a slotted spoon to the prepared sheet pan. When the crumbs have cooled, place them in a medium bowl and toss with the cassia, Togarashi Salt, and orange zest; set aside.

**3** Drain the sweetbreads and rinse them under cold water to remove any excess blood. Bring a large pot of well-salted water to a boil over medium-high heat. Add the sweetbreads and cook for 15 minutes. Meanwhile, prepare a sheet pan by lining it with paper towels. When the sweetbreads are done cooking, transfer to the prepared pan to drain and cool. Once they're cool enough to handle, remove the outer layer (this part is very tough and chewy) and any visible veins, then cut the sweetbreads into 1-inch nuggets.

**4** While the sweetbreads cook, make General Tso's Sauce: Combine the soy sauce, calamansi juice, gochujang paste, sugar, and sesame oil in a medium saucepan over

medium-high heat. Cook, stirring occasionally, until the sugar dissolves and the sauce has reduced and thickened, about 5 minutes. Transfer to a blender and purée until smooth; set aside.

5 When you're ready to fry the sweetbreads, put the flour in a medium bowl and dredge the sweetbreads until coated, shaking to remove any excess. Pour enough oil into a large pot to coat the bottom and heat over medium-high heat. Line a sheet pan with paper towels and put it by the stove to hold the sweetbreads as they come out of the oil.

6 When the oil is hot, add the sweetbreads to the pan, working in batches so you don't overcrowd them. Fry the sweetbreads, turning as needed, until golden brown on all sides, about 4 to 5 minutes total. Using a slotted spoon, carefully remove the sweetbreads from the oil and drain them on the prepared sheet pan.

7 To serve, put the sweetbread nuggets in a large bowl, drizzle with General Tso's Sauce, toss to glaze well, and sprinkle with the Cassia Breadcrumbs.

Calamansi is a citrus fruit with a vibrant flavor—the juice tends to be quite sour, but the peel is often sweet. Calamansi is very common in the Philippines, though it's used in many Asian cuisines. It's definitely an ingredient worth searching out, but if you can't find it readily, don't panic—you can still make my General Tso's Sweetbreads. Swap in lemon juice instead—it's a perfectly good substitute.

# Fried Maple-Glazed Bacon

Serves: 4   Time: About 30 minutes   Flavors: Salty/Smoky/Sweet

This sweet tempura-style dish isn't just for breakfast. Personally, I'd serve this as an entrée with something acidic like my Sweet and Sour Pickles (page 116), as a snack sprinkled with Togarashi Salt (page 53), or even chopped and sprinkled over vanilla ice cream for dessert.

½ pound smoked bacon, thickly cut
¼ cup maple syrup
¼ cup light soy sauce
3 tablespoons Worcestershire sauce

grapeseed oil
¼ cup all-purpose flour
⅓ cup water

1 Put the bacon in medium saucepan over medium-high heat and cook until it's just beginning to color, 3 to 4 minutes. Add the maple syrup, soy sauce, and Worcestershire sauce and continue to cook, stirring occasionally, until the sauce has reduced and the bacon is completely glazed, 3 to 4 minutes.  Remove the pan from the heat and let sit at room temperature.

2 Pour enough oil into a large pot to come about 3 inches up the sides. Turn the heat to high and bring to 325°F, as measured by a deep-fry or candy thermometer. Meanwhile, line a sheet pan with paper towels and put it by the stove to hold the bacon as it comes out of the oil.

3 While the oil heats, combine the flour and water in a medium bowl and mix well. When the oil is ready, dip the bacon pieces in the batter, add them to the pot, and fry until golden and crisp, 3 to 5 minutes. Use a slotted spoon to carefully transfer to the prepared sheet pan to drain any excess oil. Serve immediately.

# Ramen
## with Spam Broth

Serves: 4   Time: About 45 minutes   Flavors: Salty/Umami/Nutty

Spam is my idea of retro cool. When mixed with the right ingredients it offers up a complex flavor that makes this noodle soup totally awesome. I'm not shy about using it and you shouldn't be either. If you can't find Spam, swap in half a pound of salted ham.

one 12-ounce can Spam
4 cups water
2 tablespoons fish sauce
2 fresh thyme sprigs

¼ teaspoon kosher salt
2 tablespoons toasted sesame oil
2 tablespoons Togarashi Salt (page 53)
8 ounces ramen noodles (page 24)

1 In a medium saucepan with a lid, combine the Spam, water, fish sauce, thyme, and salt over low heat. Cook for 20 minutes, or until the Spam has totally broken down and the flavors have melded.

2 Turn off the heat, add the sesame oil and Togarashi Salt to the pan, cover, and let steep for 10 minutes. Using a fine sieve, strain the mixture and return it to the pan to keep hot.

3 Meanwhile, bring a large pot of well-salted water to a boil. Add the ramen noodles and cook until just tender, about 2 minutes; drain the noodles. To serve, divide the noodles evenly among 4 bowls and ladle the hot broth on top.

I love homemade noodles, but sometimes it's just not practical to make them—if you're in a rush or just don't have the energy, pick up good-quality packaged ramen. Asian markets almost always carry a good selection and nowadays most grocery stores have something that will work too.

# Flaked Cod Fish Bacalao with Green Olive and Tomato Stew

**Serves: 4    Time: 1 hour    Flavors: Salty/Briny/Herbaceous**

This dish is in memory of my Aunt Carmen—she used to make it when I was a child and whenever I cook it, the flavors and aromas totally remind me of her. The funny thing is, the first time I made this myself I didn't even have the recipe; I just remembered watching her make it and knew how it should come together. I miss you, Aunt Carmen.

¼ cup olive oil
1 pound salted cod, soaked in water for 2 to 4 hours and drained
one 15-ounce can plum tomatoes
¼ cup water
½ cup green olives, pitted

2 red Thai chiles, chopped
2 fresh thyme sprigs
1 fresh bay leaf
¼ cup red wine vinegar
1 cup diced celery
3 tablespoons capers
¼ teaspoon kosher salt

**1** Put the olive oil in a large saucepan over medium-high heat. When it's hot, reduce the heat to low, add the cod, and cook for about 5 minutes, using a wooden spoon to break the fish up as it cooks.

**2** Add the tomatoes, water, olives, chiles, thyme, and bay leaf and cook over low heat for another 15 minutes, then add the vinegar, celery, capers, and salt. Raise the heat and bring the mixture to a boil, then reduce the heat to a simmer and cook for another 15 minutes, stirring occasionally. Taste for seasoning and serve the stew over white rice.

# Slow-Cooked "Canned" Tuna

Serves: 4   Time: About 1 hour   Flavors: Salty/Spicy/Herbaceous

The inspiration for this recipe hit me while I was staring into my kitchen cupboard one day. Looking at a can of tuna, I was struck by the idea of creating a dish with that familiar flaky texture, but with the richness, succulence, and subtlety of great-quality fish. So I took beautiful yellowfin tuna, poached it in oil until I could flake it with a spoon, and mixed it with some spicy Asian tartar sauce. And here it is—something totally fresh yet quietly familiar too. Serve this on a bed of greens or spooned onto slices of rye bread.

1½ cups grapeseed oil
2 fresh thyme sprigs
1 pound Yellowfin tuna, from the eye
   with no bloodline (see Box)

Asian Tartar Sauce
1 tablespoon sugar
2 tablespoons seasoned rice wine
   vinegar

¼ cup Sriracha sauce
1 cup mayonnaise
2 teaspoons kosher salt
¼ cup minced celery
¼ cup minced red onion
¼ cup chopped scallion
¼ cup chopped fresh cilantro
½ avocado, peeled and chopped

**1** Place the oil and thyme in a large saucepan over medium heat. Once the oil just begins to simmer, reduce the heat to low and cook for 20 minutes to infuse the oil with the herb's flavor.

**2** Put the tuna in the oil and cook, rotating every 10 minutes or so, until it is completely cooked through, about 30 minutes total—you want the exterior of the tuna to turn opaque. Remove from the oil and set aside to cool.

**3** While the tuna cooks, make the Asian Tartar Sauce: In a small bowl, combine the sugar and vinegar and stir until the sugar dissolves. Add the Sriracha sauce, mayonnaise, salt, celery, red onion, scallion, cilantro, and avocado and mix gently to keep the avocado pieces intact.

**4** Use a spoon to flake the cooled tuna and put it in a large bowl. Add the Asian Tartar Sauce and toss lightly to combine.

When you select fresh tuna you want meat closer to the head of the tuna than the tail. This section of the fish tends to have less nerve endings and sinew and will be much more tender.

# Salted Pine
# Nut Toffee

**Serves: 4   Time: About 1 hour    Flavors: Salty/Sweet/Nutty**

My grandfather, after whom I was named, used to take me to Mets games when I was little. One of my most vibrant memories of those games was the salted nuts they sold in the stands—they were my favorite. This dessert is my interpretation of the salty nuts I used to share with my grandfather. Sweetened up with a buttery, creamy caramel, this is absolutely mind-blowing with ice cream.

**1 cup pine nuts**
**¼ cup sugar**
**2 teaspoons kosher salt**

**3 tablespoons heavy cream**
**2 tablespoons unsalted butter**

**1** In a medium saucepan over medium heat, toast the pine nuts until golden, 1 to 2 minutes. Add the sugar and cook, stirring occasionally, until it begins to melt and caramelize, 4 to 5 minutes. Add the salt and heavy cream—it will bubble up profusely. Once the bubbles dissipate, add the butter; reduce the heat to medium-low, and continue to cook for 2 minutes, or until it reaches the consistency of thick cream and coats the back of a spoon.

**2** Pour the mixture out onto a sheet pan and let stand at room temperature until it solidifies slightly and becomes chewy. To serve, cut into bite-size pieces.

# Sake and Cheddar
## Cheese Sauce

**Serves: 4   Time: About 20 minutes   Flavors: Salty/Sweet/Astringent**

Cheese sauce is one of my guilty pleasures. Whether it's for dipping barbecue-flavored chips during a football game or drizzling on hot dogs at a summer cookout, sometimes cheese just needs to be oozy and warm. My version is both of those things, but it's also a bit sophisticated—jazzed up with sake and a bit of Togarashi Salt for some spice. Amazing.

1 cup heavy cream
1 cup grated Cheddar cheese
¼ cup grated or chopped American cheese

2 teaspoons sugar
½ teaspoon kosher salt
2 teaspoons Togarashi Salt (page 53)
¼ cup sake

**1** Put the heavy cream in a medium saucepan over medium heat, bring to a low simmer, and cook gently for 4 to 5 minutes; do not allow it to come to a boil or it will become grainy. Stir in the cheeses and cook, stirring, until melted.

**2** Add the sugar, salt, and Togarashi Salt to the pan and continue cooking for another minute, until everything is thoroughly combined. Add the sake and cook for 2 minutes to burn off some of the alcohol. Transfer to a blender and purée until smooth and luscious. Serve immediately or refrigerate in an airtight container for up to a week and reheat before using.

Tuna Tartare with Chipolte Vinaigrette

Sloppy Ho Chi Minh

Tangy Ribs with Tamarind Glaze

Sautéed Duck Breast with Pancetta and Cumin-Onion Jam

Charred Octopus with Chorizo Oil and Jalapeño Pickled Onions

Asian Barbecue Sauce with Smoked Chiles
and Pineapple

Charred Mushrooms with Smoked Bacon and CorianderVinaigrette

Sake Sangria with Lemongrass, Lychee, and Ginger

# Smoky 3

# Smoky | The Meal of My Life

I was walking down a traffic-riddled street in the heart of Hanoi on a steamy August evening. The noise was relentless: car horns blaring, rickshaw drivers yelling, the constant hum of a foreign language. The sounds and smells and the feel of the air—it was invigorating. I felt like my entire nervous system was on overload as I tried to take it all in. There was more exhaust in the air than the sensual aromas I had imagined, but that didn't matter. I just kept thinking to myself, "I'm here, I'm in the land of sweet-salty-sour." Then I found it: An ancient, tarnished old door announcing the entrance to what I had been told was the place to experience true Vietnamese food at its most authentic: Cha Ca La Vong.

I pushed on the door, feeling the grain of the wood on the tips of my fingers, and walked in. I headed up a creaky staircase, the walls adorned with pictures that told the history of this fabled restaurant, and I felt like I was climbing into the attic of an old haunted house. Only here I wasn't confronted by cobwebs or the musty smell of stagnant air, but by a delicious aroma that lingered—the intoxicating scent of years and years of spicy, fragrant meals—rich, robust flavors that seemed to have made themselves part of the walls.

I walked into the main room of Cha Ca La Vong and was immediately directed to a table with a white paper tablecloth and a charcoal grill burning in the center. There was smoke in the air and I felt like I had stumbled into an Al Pacino movie—then a waiter slammed a Tiger beer down in front of me; it was cool and foamy and dripping with perspiration. I knew I had come to the perfect place.

Asian humidity is insane; it's thick and sweet, and that night it felt like it was seeping in through the windows as I sat there sipping my beer and waiting to eat. But then the air changed. I felt a searing heat from behind me and before I had a chance to figure out what it was, another waiter placed a bubbling pot in front of me, a small kettle of turmeric oil—brilliant gold in color and percolating as little pieces of crisp fish danced in the fat. I was already totally intrigued when he came back with two bunches of fresh dill and one of cilantro. I must have looked up at him with a thoroughly confused expression, because he suddenly took the dill and almost threw it into the oil—crackling and spattering.

I was totally taken aback. It wasn't the noise of the blistering oil, the fat that was quickly staining my shirt, or even the burning feeling on my arms, none of that even registered—it was all about the dill. The aroma was insane; I felt like I had been hit in the face, the scent was so powerful. I was almost dizzy, stunned by the roaring wave of the natural essence that enveloped me. I honestly felt like it lifted me to a place I'd never been before, like I had been drugged by its potency. Until this moment I hadn't even known that dill was used in Southeast Asian cooking, and suddenly it was all around me. I was mystified; how did I not know this, how had I not experienced this flavor in all its brilliance before? I just couldn't get my head around it; I was completely captivated.

The next thing I knew the waiter was dropping a bowl of vermicelli noodles with peanut sauce, bean sprouts, Thai basil, cilantro, and mint in front of me. Then he reached over and spooned some of the fish and dill into the noodles, stood back, and smiled as if to say, "Now eat." And man, did I.

Right there and then I knew this was a different kind of meal. It was a full-on sensory experience: the smell of the dill, the sound of the oil spitting and splattering, the touch of the creamy peanut sauce on my tongue, and the flavor of all those herbs and other ingredients— each holding their own yet blending perfectly together. It was at that moment that I knew my decision to leave a phenomenal job working for Jean-Georges in New York to experience this was all worth it. I had already, before even finishing that meal, learned more about the diversity of ingredients than I had in all my years of education and working. It wasn't just transporting—it was transcendent.

# Tuna Tartare
## with Chipotle Vinaigrette

Serves: 6 to 8    Time: About 15 minutes    Flavors: Smoky/Spicy/Salty

When I was travelling in Vietnam, I reached for a lettuce wrap every chance I got—they're light and crisp, and there's something sexy about eating with your hands. So when I got home I decided to marry tuna tartare with a bit of spice and wrap it all up in a lettuce leaf. Add some mint, Thai basil, or cilantro and you have the perfect hors d'oeuvre in no time. Not feeling the love for lettuce? This tuna is also incredible on top of good-quality potato chips or toasted bread. Just be sure to get #1 Grade sashimi-quality tuna.

2 dried chipotle chiles, stems removed
6 tablespoons grapeseed oil
½ teaspoon kosher, salt plus more cas needed
2 tablespoons gochujang paste (see Box)
2 tablespoons fish sauce

3 tablespoons seasoned rice wine vinegar
1 tablespoon toasted sesame oil
2 cups chopped sashimi-grade tuna
2 tablespoons finely chopped shallot
1 head Bibb lettuce, leaves separated

1 In a small dry sauté pan, lightly toast the chipotle until the essential oils are extracted, about 2 minutes; let cool. Put the chipotle in a blender with 3 tablespoons of the oil, ½ teaspoon of the salt, the gochujang paste, fish sauce, vinegar, and sesame oil and purée until smooth. Chill in the refrigerator for at least 10 minutes.

2 Meanwhile, lightly toss the tuna with the shallots and the remaining 3 tablespoons oil and season with salt to taste. Drizzle the tuna with the chipotle vinaigrette and serve wrapped in the lettuce leaves.

Gochujang is a Korean fermented chile paste, traditionally aged in clay pots. It's used as a condiment in many Korean dishes, including Bibimbap, and is available at Asian markets.

# Sloppy Ho
## Chi Minh

Serves: 6    Time: 30 minutes    Flavors: Smoky/Spicy/Sweet

Inspired by the flavors of Vietnam, this is my interpretation of an old-fashioned Sloppy Joe—only much more exotic. The garlic, ginger, cumin, and cloves make it wonderfully aromatic; the shrimp paste gives it a touch of sweetness; and the gochujang paste offers just a hint of heat. Toss all this on a buttery brioche roll and it's like a ticket to Ho Chi Minh City without any of the jet lag. Awesome.

2 tablespoons unsalted butter
2 tablespoons olive oil
2 tablespoons chopped garlic
1 tablespoon chopped ginger
1 tablespoon shrimp paste
1 pound ground beef
3 tablespoons sugar
¼ cup gochujang paste (see Box, page 70)

2 teaspoons cumin, toasted and ground
4 cloves, toasted and ground
1½ cups good-quality chicken stock
6 brioche rolls
1 cup iceberg lettuce, shredded
6 slices Cheddar cheese

**1** Put the butter and oil in a large saucepan over medium heat. When the butter has melted and the oil is hot, add the garlic and ginger and cook until aromatic, about 2 minutes.  Add the shrimp paste, reduce the heat to low, and cook for another 2 minutes.

**2** Add the ground beef, sugar, gochujang paste, cumin, and cloves to the pan and continue cooking, stirring occasionally, until the meat is thoroughly browned, another 5 minutes. Add the chicken stock and cook for another 10 minutes, or until the liquid has reduced and the meat is completely glazed.

**3** Meanwhile, toast the brioche rolls and mound ¼ cup of lettuce on the bottom of each roll. Spoon a generous portion of the ground beef on top of the lettuce, add a slice of cheese, and top each sandwich with the other half of the bun to serve.

# Tangy Ribs
## with Tamarind Glaze

Serves: 4 to 6   Time: About 3½ hours   Flavors: Smoky/Spicy/Sour

In its pure form, tamarind comes in a pod—the fruit itself is fleshy and is usually processed into a paste or a pulp. For this recipe, I'm using the paste form, which you can find at Asian markets and even some larger grocery stores these days. If you have more time on your hands, you can use the pulp—just know that you need to combine it with water and boil it down to create a paste. Either way, the tangy, tart, sour flavor of the tamarind marries this American staple with the sensual flavors of Southeast Asia.

4 quarts water
1½ cups tamarind paste
3 cups ketchup
1 cup packed brown sugar
¼ cup Sriracha sauce
¼ cup gochujang paste (see Box, page 70)

1 cup red wine vinegar
1 cup dried pineapple
¼ cup chipotle chiles in adobo sauce
5 pounds St. Louis ribs (see Box)

1 Preheat the oven to 300°F.

2 Put the water, tamarind, ketchup, brown sugar, Sriracha sauce, gochujang paste, vinegar, dried pineapple, and chipotles with their sauce in a large saucepan set over medium-high heat. Bring to a boil, reduce to a simmer, and cook for about 5 minutes, until thoroughly combined. Transfer to a blender and purée until smooth.

3 Place the ribs in a roasting pan and pour the puréed liquid over the ribs. Cover the pan with foil and place it in the oven. Cook for 2½ to 3 hours, checking after an hour to make sure the liquid hasn't evaporated. If the liquid level seems low, add a cup or two of water as needed to keep the ribs submerged during cooking.

4 When the ribs are fork-tender, transfer to a sheet pan, and carefully strain the braising liquid through a fine sieve into a large saucepan. Put the liquid over medium-high heat and reduce until it's the consistency of a sauce, 10 to 15 minutes.

5 Turn the oven to broil. Brush the ribs with the sauce and broil for 2 to 3 minutes to lacquer the exterior, making sure they don't burn. Serve immediately.

St. Louis ribs have the rib tips, sternum bone, and cartilage removed, so what you're left with is a very rectangular shaped slab. This cut is ideal because not only does it fit nicely in a roasting pan, but it also helps ensure even cooking.

# Sautéed Duck Breast
# with Pancetta and Cumin-Onion Jam

Serves: 4    Time: About 1 hour    Flavors: Smoky/Astringent/Sweet

This dish is all about contrasts: The sweetness of the onions balances out the saltiness of the pancetta. The rich, gamey duck plays off the smoky pork. The nutty flavor of the cumin enlivens the tanginess of the onions. I could go on and on—it's magical . . .

Cumin-Onion Jam
2 tablespoons unsalted butter
2 tablespoons grapeseed oil
2 tablespoons cumin seeds
2 cups thinly sliced onions
¼ cup sugar
½ teaspoon kosher salt
3 tablespoons chopped fresh Thai basil

4 small Peking or Muscovy duck
  breasts
2 tablespoons kosher salt
2 tablespoons grapeseed oil
8 slices pancetta, about ⅛-inch thick
  and cut in half
2 fresh thyme sprigs
freshly ground black pepper

**1** Make the Cumin-Onion Jam: Put the butter and oil in a large sauté pan over medium-high heat. When the butter has melted and the oil is hot, add the cumin seeds and cook until fragrant, 2 to 3 minutes. Add the onions, sugar, and salt, reduce the heat to medium, and cook until the onions are tender, golden, and the consistency of jam, about 15 minutes. Let cool, then mix in the basil and set aside.

**2** Pat the duck breasts dry with paper towels. If you're using Muscovy duck, slash the skin diagonally with a sharp knife (being careful not to cut through the meat). Season the breasts well with salt. Put a large sauté pan over medium-high heat and add the breasts skin side down. Reduce the heat and cook until all the fat is rendered, 20 to 25 minutes. When the skin is crisp, pour off most of the fat and reserve it (see Box), leaving just enough to coat the bottom of the pan. Flip the breasts and cook for 5 minutes, or until medium-rare. Let rest on a cutting board.

**3** Meanwhile, heat the oil in a medium sauté pan. Add the pancetta, thyme, and a few grinds of pepper; cook until the pancetta begins to color, 8 to 10 minutes.

**4** To serve, slice the duck breasts diagonally, lay some of the pancetta alongside the duck, and top with a generous serving of the Cumin-Onion Jam.

Duck fat is amazingly flavorful and adds a deliciously decadent edge to everything from French fries to fried rice. After you render the fat, pour it into a bowl and let it cool. Then transfer it to an airtight container and keep it in the fridge or freezer for up to 3 months. Anytime you feel like giving something an extra bump of flavor, use it instead of butter or oil.

# Charred Octopus with Chorizo Oil
## and Jalapeño Pickled Onions

Serves: 4    Time: About 2 hours    Flavors: Smoky/Spicy/Briny

Octopus can get tough if it's overcooked. In this recipe I treat it gently by letting it marinate with fresh herbs (like a tea). This technique infuses the octopus with flavor while also preserving its tenderness. The combo of the smoky Spanish chorizo, the briny olives, and the hot chiles reminds me of the great tapas I've enjoyed in San Sebastian, Spain. Perfecto!

Jalapeño Pickled Onions
½ cup seasoned rice wine vinegar
3 tablespoons sugar
1 jalapeño chile, thinly sliced
¼ cup thinly sliced red onion

4 cups water
½ cup red wine vinegar
¼ cup plus 2 tablespoons olive oil

4 fresh thyme sprigs
2 fresh bay leaves
2 teaspoons kosher salt
1 pound whole octopus
¼ cup diced Spanish chorizo
¼ cup diced celery
3 tablespoons green olives

1 First make the Jalapeño Pickled Onions: Put the vinegar and sugar in a medium bowl and stir to dissolve. Add the jalapeño and onion and let sit at room temperature for at least 30 minutes or up to 24 hours in the fridge.

2 Meanwhile, put the water in a large saucepan along with the vinegar, ¼ cup of the oil, the thyme, bay leaves, and salt and bring to a boil. Add the octopus and remove the pan from the heat, letting it rest for 15 to 20 minutes before placing the pan in the refrigerator to chill for at least 1 hour.

3 When fully chilled, transfer the octopus to a cutting board. Peel off the outer skin and discard. Cut the octopus into 2-inch pieces and set aside.

4 Put the remaining 2 tablespoons of oil in a large, deep pan over high heat. When it's hot, add the chorizo and cook for about 5 minutes, or until the fat has rendered and the meat begins to color. Add the octopus to the pan and cook, turning occasionally, until all sides are charred, 2 to 3 minutes.

5 Add the celery and olives to the pan and cook for about 1 minute—the celery should still be crisp on the inside. Spoon the octopus mixture into bowls and garnish with the Jalapeño Pickled Onions.

# Asian Barbecue Sauce
# with Smoked Chiles and Pineapple

**Makes: 3 cups    Time: About 20 minutes    Flavors: Smoky/Sweet/Spicy**

This is another sauce I love to use and abuse. If I could, I'd take a bath in this stuff—seriously, it's that good. Brush it on chicken, beef, or pork. Make a killer shrimp cocktail. Dish it up with pancakes and maple syrup. Like I said: Use and abuse!

1 cup packed brown sugar
1 cup dried pineapple
1½ cups red wine vinegar
2 cups ketchup
1 cup gochujang paste (see Box,
  page 70)

¼ cup Sriracha sauce
3 tablespoons chipotle chiles
  in adobo sauce
1 tablespoon kosher salt

**1** Put the sugar in a medium saucepan over medium-high heat and cook, stirring frequently, until it melts, 3 to 4 minutes. Add the pineapple and cook until completely soft, another 5 to 8 minutes.

**2** Add the vinegar, increase the heat to high, and bring to a boil; continue cooking until the vinegar has reduced by about a third, then add the ketchup, gochujang paste, Sriracha sauce, chipotles with their sauce, and salt. Cook over medium-low heat until slightly thickened and thoroughly combined, 8 to 10 minutes. Transfer to a blender and purée until smooth. Use as desired or place in an airtight container and refrigerate for up to 3 months.

# Charred Mushrooms with Smoked
## Bacon and CorianderVinaigrette

**Serves: 6 to 8    Time: About 30 minutes    Flavors: Smoky/Earthy/Acidic**

These magic mushrooms come alive, thanks to the smokiness of the bacon and the tanginess of the warm vinaigrette. The accent of the cracked coriander provides a textural contrast with the meaty mushrooms and gives the whole dish a floral, citrus note that's just awesome.

3 tablespoons olive oil
¼ cup smoked bacon cut into ½-inch
  pieces
2 cups stemmed and halved oyster
  mushrooms
2 cup stemmed and quartered shiitake
  mushrooms
2 cups stemmed, halved, and cubed
  trumpet mushrooms

2 teaspoons kosher salt
2 teaspoons coriander seeds, cracked
2 tablespoons sugar
½ cup seasoned rice wine vinegar
1 tablespoon fresh thyme leaves
2 teaspoons chopped fresh rosemary

**1** Put 1 tablespoon of the oil in a large sauté pan over medium-high heat. Add the bacon and cook until it has rendered some of its fat and is beginning to brown, 4 to 5 minutes. Use a slotted spoon to remove the bacon from the fat and set aside.

**2** Add the remaining 2 tablespoons of oil to the pan with the rendered bacon fat and add the mushrooms. Sprinkle with the salt and cook, stirring frequently to make sure the mushrooms brown on all sides but retain their meatiness, 3 to 4 minutes.

**3** When the mushrooms are beginning to crisp on the edges, add the bacon back to the pan, toss to combine, and reduce the heat to low while the flavors meld, another 2 minutes. Remove from the heat and set aside.

**4** Put the cracked coriander seeds in a small saucepan over medium heat and toast until just aromatic, about 2 minutes. Add the sugar, raise the heat to medium-high, and let melt, 3 to 4 minutes.  Add the vinegar and deglaze the pan. When the mixture is thoroughly combined and just beginning to thicken, add the thyme and rosemary, mix well, and remove from the heat.

**5** Pour the warm vinaigrette over the mushroom-bacon mixture, toss well, and serve.

# Sake Sangria
## with Lemongrass, Lychee, and Ginger

Serves: 4 to 6  Time: 15 minutes  Flavors: Smoky/Sweet/Herbaceous

Japan meets Spain in this globally inspired cocktail. I promise you can't drink just one, so be careful! And be sure to give the ginger, lemongrass, and herbs time to infuse the sake and wine—you really want to taste all the different flavors to get the full experience.

2 cups sake
1 bottle red wine
½ cup agave nectar
one 2-inch piece ginger, sliced
1 lemongrass stalk, smashed
4 allspice berries
1 fresh rosemary sprig

2 fresh mint sprigs
½ cup peeled and pitted lychee
 fruit (if canned, drained
 and rinsed)
fleur de sel or other high
 quality salt

In a pitcher, combine the sake, wine, and agave nectar and stir well to blend. Add the ginger, lemongrass, allspice, rosemary, and mint and let sit for at least 1 hour to infuse the liquid with the flavor of the aromatics. Add the lychee to the pitcher and serve over ice. Garnish each glass with a pinch of the fleur de sel.

Tuna Ribbons with Candied Wasabi

# Frisée Salad with Yuzu-Thyme Vinaigrette

Green Papaya Salad with Candied Tamarind Vinaigrettte

# Grilled Tofu in Ponzu Marinade with Crispy Shallots

# Tuna Mole

## Broccoli Rabe with Aleppo Pepper

Mustard Seed Potato Salad with Pickled Shallots and Dill

# Southeast Asian Mojito with Thai Basil and Mint

## Curry Powder "My Way"

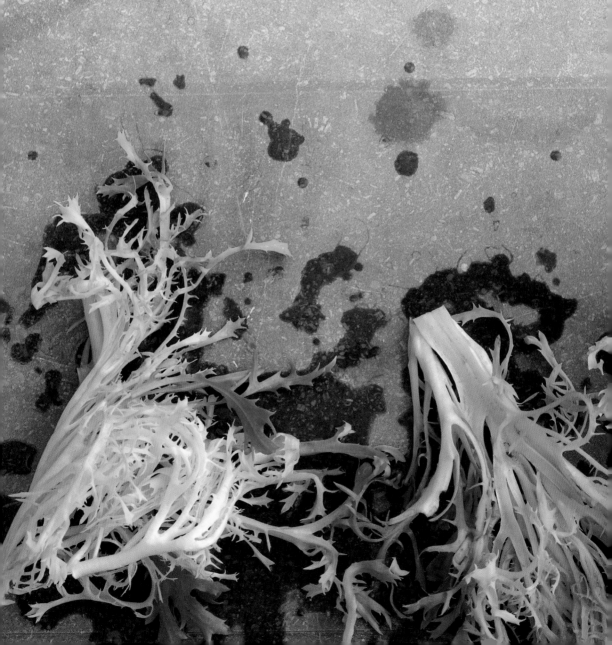

# Bitter 4

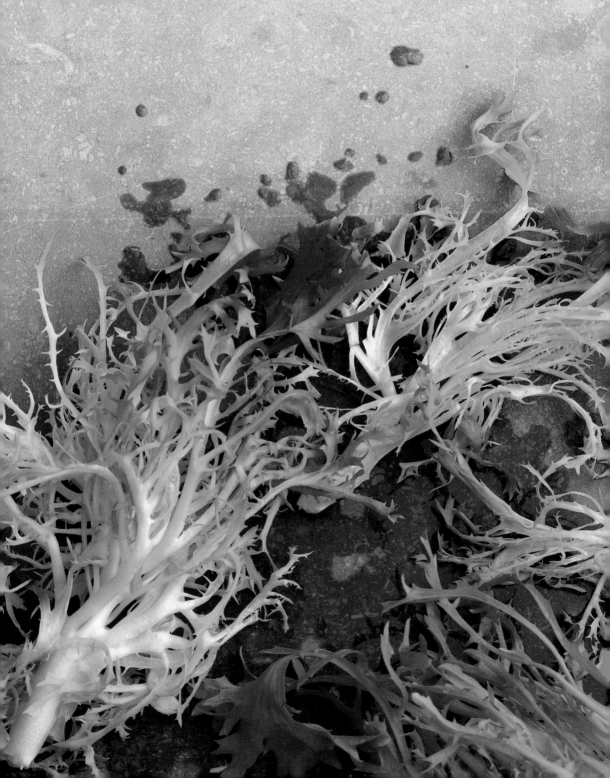

# Bitter | Live and Learn, Learn and Live

I think everyone has an experience that they wish they could go back and do over again—and do differently. For me, that experience was my first restaurant, Yumcha. It's not that I'm not proud of what we built at Yumcha—I am. It was an amazing restaurant for the short time that it was open, but I'm still saddened by the way everything went down. For years I've wanted to tell this story, but I didn't know what people would think. I'm at a place now where I feel good about this; it's what happened and I learned a ton from it. If nothing else, it's important for me to share this in the hope that someone else learns from it too.

At the time, I was working with Jean-Georges when the opportunity to open Yumcha came up. It was a difficult decision to leave my mentor, and I had very mixed feelings about it. But the chance to create my own restaurant, to develop my own vision was too tempting—I had to take the risk. The long version of what happened is complicated and full of conflict. This is the short story; the one that has helped me grow as a chef and a person, and that I hold as the truth.

After spending about three months of my life working eighteen- and twenty-hour days to create a contemporary Chinese restaurant like no other, it finally opened. Some of the world's greatest chefs were coming to eat at Yumcha: Alain Ducasse, Paul Bocuse, Gray Kunz, Jean-Georges all came in—the best of the best. Dana Cowin from Food & Wine magazine showed up, Adam Platt wrote a rave in New York Magazine; the press was incredible and reviews were sick right off the bat. We were on the cusp of something fantastic and everyone in the kitchen could feel it. The food we were making was edgy and exciting: Asian flavors fused with French preparations in a way that was really fresh and sexy. The room was stunning, very elegant with black lacquered surfaces and a gleaming open kitchen. The chefs wore pinstripes and were all decked out in tall toques—it was a full sensory experience. There were lines around the block to get in. It was everything we'd all worked for and everything I'd hoped for. But it didn't last long.

My relationship with the owner became stressful as our ideas about Yumcha diverged. Some of it was management stuff, some was just personal style, but it was starting to become obvious that we had different visions. None of the details are terribly important, but our direction was at stake and to me that was huge. Finally, the friction between us became palpable in meetings; it was so bad that I knew we had to get beyond it. We had to talk.

One day I asked him if we could speak outside. I told him what I was feeling: How much Yumcha meant to me, how awesome our trajectory was. I remember saying, "We have this amazing product. We really need to make this work." The conversation escalated, we argued, voices were raised, and it got intense. We went our separate ways, ostensibly to cool down. Then, about two hours before that night's service, he called me back outside. We tried talking, but it was too late. He told me to leave. I had no idea how it had gotten so far out of control so fast, but I knew that what had been a fractured relationship had just broken, irrevocably.

I went downstairs to the kitchen and saw my staff working away in perfect unison toward that night's service. They looked up when they saw me come in and I could barely speak. I just said, "Guys, I've been asked to leave." Everyone was in disbelief. But what could I do? I left.

I was walking down Bedford Street, about a block from the restaurant, when I realized there were people following me. At first I didn't connect who they were, this group trailing a block behind. Then it was as if a fog cleared—my staff, my team had walked out, had left the kitchen to follow me. By no means would I ever have asked or wanted them to sacrifice their jobs for me, but I can't deny I was touched. Then we noticed some of the wait staff as well; all of us walking together away from this place we'd worked so hard to build. It was incredible, this demonstration of loyalty; it was such an honor to know that these people who had also believed so deeply in Yumcha, who had put so much of themselves into it, were willing to walk away in support of me.

The restaurant closed that night. They tried to reopen a week or so later, but it didn't work. Our moment had passed.

# It was everything we'd all worked for and everything I'd hoped for. But it didn't last long.

At first I was torn up inside about Yumcha, bitter, angry, and heartbroken. It was so perfect, so pristine in concept and execution for the brief time it was alive—which is how I thought of it, as a living, breathing entity. But with time I began to see the whole experience as a lesson I needed to learn. I was naïve, blinded by my own passion and ambition. I had been ready for the challenge, but it wasn't the right situation for me. Though no one could have convinced me of that back then. I had to find out for myself.

When the staff followed me down the street on that last night, it was that sign of loyalty, dedication, and sacrifice that allowed me see the light in what was a pretty dark experience. I knew then what was most important: I had built a great team, together we had built a great restaurant, and regardless of the outcome, I had poured my heart into something I believed in.

# Tuna Ribbons
## with Candied Wasabi

Serves: 4 to 6    Time: About 2½ hours    Flavors: Bitter/Sweet/Astringent

You could say that this dish showcases a little of my Italian side, as these ribbons resemble freshly cut fettuccine. Wasabi is a Japanese root that's very pungent and strong in flavor. This recipe is a perfect example of how I think about pairing flavors: The strong wasabi is tamed by the sweetness of the sugar with which it is candied, the acidity of the vinegar in the dressing helps refresh your palate, while the umami flavor of the soy sauce creates that yummy factor we're always going for.

¼ cup plus 2 teaspoons sugar
¼ cup wasabi powder
1 tablespoon water
1 pound #1 grade sashimi-quality tuna
1½ teaspoons kosher salt

3 tablespoons olive oil
6 tablespoons light soy sauce
¼ cup seasoned rice wine vinegar
fresh cilantro leaves

**1** In a medium bowl, combine ¼ cup of the sugar with the wasabi powder and water. Spread the mixture onto a sheet pan (it should resemble streusel topping) and let it dry at room temperature for at least 2 hours or until completely dry. When the candy is completely dry, crumble it into pieces about the size of peas.

**2** Cut the tuna lengthwise into ¼-inch-thick pieces, then slice each piece to form ribbons about ⅛ inch thick. Put the ribbons in a medium bowl, sprinkle with the salt, toss with the olive oil, and place in the fridge to chill.

**3** In a small bowl, combine the soy sauce, vinegar, and the remaining 2 teaspoons sugar and mix until the sugar is completely dissolved.

**4** To serve, toss the chilled tuna ribbons with the soy sauce dressing, top with a few pieces of the wasabi candy, and garnish with a cilantro leaf.

# Frisée Salad
## with Yuzu-Thyme Vinaigrette

Serves: 4   Time: About 15 minutes   Flavors: Bitter/Acidic/Sweet

I love classic salade Lyonnaise, so I wanted to create my own version—with an Asian twist. Yuzu is a highly prized Japanese citrus fruit with a lovely well-rounded flavor. Combined with the creaminess of the egg yolk and the lightly salted whites, this tangy dressing brightens up the earthy greens in a fresh, new way.

**4 heads frisée lettuce**
**3 tablespoons olive oil**
**¼ cup yuzu juice (see Box,**
  **page 23) or lemon juice**
**1 tablespoon fresh thyme leaves**

**2 teaspoons sugar**
**kosher salt**
**1 large egg**
**freshly ground pepper**
**3 fresh dill sprigs**

**1** In a large bowl, separate the leaves of the frisée and tear into smaller pieces if desired. In a small bowl, combine 2 tablespoons of the olive oil, the yuzu juice, thyme, sugar, and a sprinkling of salt. Whisk the mixture to combine well and set aside.

**2** Put the remaining tablespoon of olive oil in a small sauté pan set over medium-high heat. When the oil is hot, crack the egg into the pan and cook until the whites are set but the yolk is still runny, about 2 minutes. Season the whites with a sprinkle of the salt and pepper.

**3** When the egg is done, lightly dress the frisée, garnish with the dill, and place the fried egg on top. To serve, slice up the egg so that it is integrated into the salad and the yolk lightly coats the greens.

# Green Papaya Salad
## with Candied Tamarind Vinaigrette

Serves: 4    Time: About 30 minutes    Flavors: Bitter/Sweet/Sour

This is one of my favorite street foods—in Bangkok, where I first tasted this dish, they toss in fresh crab, shell and all. It's a completing transporting experience: As you eat the salad you stumble on pieces of shell, their crevices filled with bright, tangy vinaigrette just begging to be sucked out. My version is vegetarian, but if you're feeling adventurous, add some beautiful blue crab (shells are totally optional).

1 cup Chinese long beans,
  cut into 3-inch pieces
2 tablespoons grapeseed oil
kosher salt
1 pound green papaya, shredded
¼ cup fresh cilantro leaves

Candied Tamarind Vinaigrette
2 tablespoons grapeseed oil
2 tablespoons thinly sliced garlic
3 Thai chiles, 2 chopped and 1 minced

½ cup candied tamarind (see Box)
¼ cup sugar
2 tablespoons chopped ginger
2 tablespoons fish sauce
3 tablespoons lime juice
kosher salt
3 tablespoons coarsely chopped
  toasted cashews

**1** Put a dry cast-iron or other heavy pan over high heat and bring it to the point of smoking. Add the long beans and cook them, turning frequently, until they're well charred on all sides but not burnt. Carefully transfer them to a medium bowl and toss them with the oil and season with salt. Chill in the refrigerator for 10 minutes.

**2** Working in batches if necessary, use a mortar and pestle to pound the papaya until it's soft and releases some of its juice (you can also wrap the papaya in a dish towel and pound it with the back of a pot—you just want to break down the fibers). Place in a large bowl, add the cilantro and long beans, and toss to combine.

**3** Make the Candied Tamarind Vinaigrette: In a small sauté pan, combine the oil and garlic and cook over medium-high heat until lightly golden, 2 to 3 minutes. Transfer to a blender along with the 2 chopped chiles, the candied tamarind, sugar, ginger, and fish sauce. Blend until smooth, then add the lime juice and blend until just combined. Season with salt as needed. To serve, drizzle the vinaigrette over the papaya mixture and garnish with the cashews and minced chiles.

I love candied tamarind—it's sort of sweet, sour, and spicy all at once. The bummer is it's not always easy to find. Candied ginger on the other hand is pretty much everywhere these days and makes a perfectly good substitute.

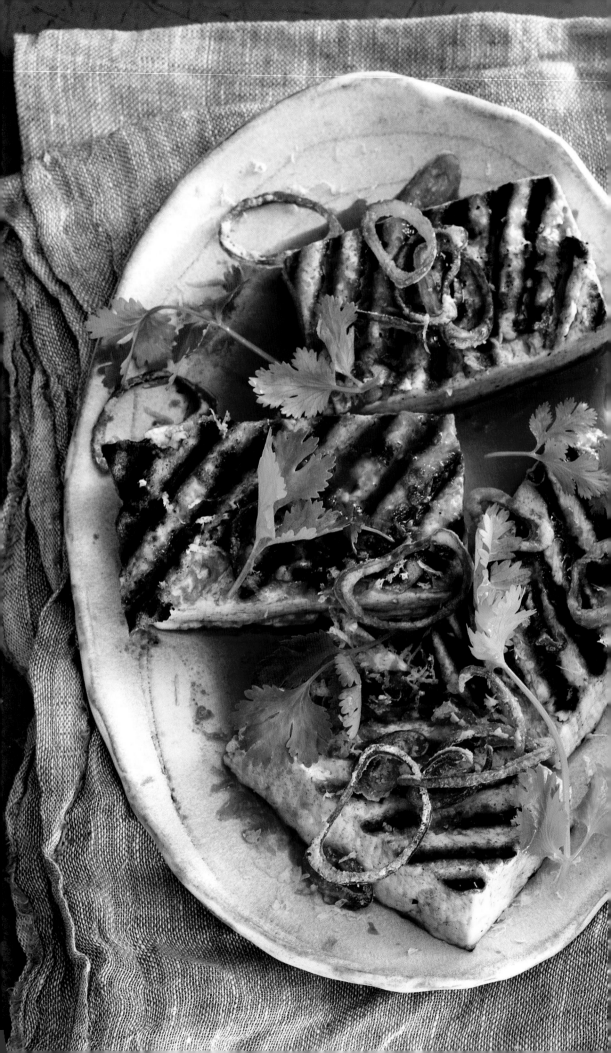

# Grilled Tofu in Ponzu Marinade
## with Crispy Shallots

Serves: 4    Time: About 1½ hours    Flavors: Bitter/Sweet/Acidic

This is great entrée, but also a delicious lunchtime or late-night snack: Toss the tofu on a brioche roll, add a dollop of mayo, and call it a day (or night, as you wish).

one 14-ounce package firm tofu
grapeseed oil
1 cup light soy sauce
¼ cup pineapple juice
¼ cup lemon juice
3 tablespoons sugar
3 tablespoons gochujang paste
  (see Box, page 70)

3 tablespoons cornstarch
¼ cup thinly sliced shallots
kosher salt
zest of 1 lemon
3 fresh cilantro sprigs

**1** Preheat a grill to high heat, or heat a grill pan over medium-high heat. Cut the tofu into four 1-inch-thick slabs and pat them dry with paper towels. Lightly brush the tofu with oil and grill on both sides until deeply charred, about 1 minute each side. Transfer to a wide, shallow dish.

**2** In a medium bowl, combine the soy sauce, pineapple juice, lemon juice, sugar, and gochujang paste and mix well.  Pour the marinade over the grilled tofu and let sit at room temperature for 1 hour.

**3** Meanwhile, pour enough oil into a small saucepan to come 1½ to 2 inches up the sides. Bring the temperature to 325°F over high heat, as measured by a deep-fry or candy thermometer. Meanwhile, line a sheet pan with paper towels and put it by the stove to hold the shallots as they come out of the oil.

**4** Put the cornstarch in a small bowl. Dredge the shallot discs in the cornstarch, shaking to remove any excess. When the oil is hot, add the shallots to the pot and cook until golden brown, about 2 minutes. Using a slotted spoon, transfer to the prepared sheet pan, let drain, and sprinkle with salt.

**5** To serve, place the tofu on a large plate, sprinkle the lemon zest on top, and sprinkle with the crispy shallots to finish. Garnish with cilantro leaves.

# Tuna Mole

This dish represents the essence of my philosophy: that simplicity is complexity. It's incredibly easy to pull together, but the combination of flavors is layered and multi-dimensional. Mole is a chocolate-based sauce; typically it's slightly bitter, slightly spicy, and has just a hint of underlying sweetness. Don't be freaked out— the combo of fish and chocolate just makes sense; the chocolate accentuates the rich, buttery texture of the tuna and the spices round out the whole experience.

½ teaspoon cumin seeds
½ teaspoon coriander seeds
4 ounces bittersweet chocolate
1 pound #1 grade sashimi-quality tuna
1½ teaspoons kosher salt
3 tablespoons olive oil

2 tablespoons gochujang paste
  (see Box, page 70)
2 limes, quartered
3 tablespoons chopped fresh cilantro

**1** In a small dry sauté pan set over low heat, lightly toast the cumin seeds and coriander seeds until the essential oils are released and the spices are aromatic, about 2 minutes. Remove the pan from the heat and let cool completely. Put the seeds in a spice grinder and grind until very fine. Set aside.

**2** Put the chocolate in a microwave-safe container. Melt in 20-second intervals in the microwave. Add the ground spices to the chocolate and stir to combine well.

**3** Cut the tuna into ¼-inch cubes, place in a medium bowl, and sprinkle with the salt. Add the oil and gochujang paste and toss gently until thoroughly combined. To serve, spoon the tuna on plates, drizzle with the melted chocolate, and garnish with lime segments and a sprinkling of the cilantro.

# Broccoli Rabe
# with Aleppo Pepper

**Serves: 4   Time: About 15 minutes   Flavors: Bitter/Sweet/Astringent**

Raising a large family out in the country, my father was passionate about feeding us as much from our own garden as possible. He just loved the idea that he was growing food to provide for the seven of us. And because my mother is Italian, he always grew an abundance of broccoli rabe. Come late fall and early winter, my mother would make this very simple, rustic dish and I always loved it.

**3 tablespoons olive oil**
**1 tablespoon thinly sliced garlic**
**2 teaspoons ground Aleppo pepper**
  **(see Box)**

**1 pound broccoli rabe, trimmed**
**1 teaspoon kosher salt**
**zest of 1 lemon**

**1** Put the olive oil in a large sauté pan over medium-high heat. When the oil is hot, add the garlic and pepper and cook, stirring frequently, for about 1 minute, until the garlic becomes aromatic and is just beginning to color.

**2** Add the broccoli rabe, season with the salt, and cover the pan with a lid (this will create steam to help wilt the broccoli rabe). Cook for about 2 minutes, until slightly wilted but still crunchy on the inside. Transfer the broccoli rabe to a large plate, and sprinkle lemon zest over the top to serve.

Aleppo pepper is a crushed chile pepper from Turkey and Syria that's found in a lot of Mediterranean and Middle Eastern cooking. It has a really robust, almost tart flavor—kind of like an ancho chile with a bit more kick. If you don't have Aleppo in the house, crushed red pepper will be a little less complex but can be substituted.

# Mustard Seed Potato Salad
## with Pickled Shallots and Dill

Serves: 4   Time: About 45 minutes   Flavors: Bitter/Acidic/Herbaceous

I'm a fiend for mustard seeds. I've even started to make my own homemade mustard. I'm just obsessed with the flavor of this spice! In this salad the peppery notes of the mustard, the creaminess of the potatoes, and the brightness of the shallots and dill are just luscious.

1 pound German Butterball or other heirloom potatoes

kosher salt

4 tablespoons (½ stick) unsalted butter

3 tablespoons yellow mustard seeds

3 tablespoons Dijon-style mustard

2 tablespoons mayonnaise

¼ cup seasoned rice wine vinegar

2 tablespoons sugar

½ cup thinly sliced shallots

3 tablespoons chopped fresh dill

1 Put the potatoes in a large pot of salted water over medium-high heat. Bring to a boil, then reduce the heat to low and simmer for 20 minutes, or until tender when pierced with a fork. Drain the potatoes. When they are cool enough to handle, peel and transfer to a large bowl; cover with plastic wrap and set aside.

2 Put the butter in a small skillet over medium heat. When the butter is melted, add the mustard seeds and cook, stirring frequently, until they burst, 1 to 2 minutes. Remove from the heat and add the mixture to the potatoes along with the mustard and mayonnaise. Use a fork to crush the potatoes and integrate all the ingredients together. Set aside in a warm spot.

3 Meanwhile, in a small bowl, combine the vinegar, sugar, and ¼ teaspoon salt and mix until the sugar and salt dissolve. Add the shallots and stir to combine.

4 To serve, stir the dill into the potato salad and spoon into bowls. Drain the shallots from the pickling liquid and top each serving with a few shallots.

# Southeast Asian Mojito
## with Thai Basil and Mint

**Serves: 4 to 6    Time: About 10 minutes    Flavors: Bitter/Sweet/Herbaceous**

Picture this: White sand, crashing waves, the smell of coconut oil in the air. Why not dazzle up the experience with this cumin-spiked mojito? I've had my fair share of these, and here's a warning: A single batch isn't gonna cut it. Double the recipe and invite some friends over to join in.

6 fresh Thai basil leaves
6 fresh mint leaves
2 tablespoons agave nectar
2 cups white rum
½ cup coconut water

3 tablespoons calamansi juice
    (see Box, page 57) or orange juice
3 tablespoons lime juice
1 teaspoon ground cumin, toasted
1 calamansi or lime, cut into slices

**1** Place the Thai basil, mint, and agave nectar in a large pitcher. Use a muddler to smash the herbs into the agave nectar and release their flavor.

**2** Add the rum, coconut water, calamansi juice, lime juice, and cumin and stir well.

**3** Fill highball glasses with ice and pour the mojito mixture over the top. Garnish with slices of calamansi or lime.

# Curry Powder
## "My Way"

**Makes: About 1 cup    Time: About 10 minutes**
**Flavors: Bitter/Earthy/Astringent**

There is no one recipe for curry powder—everyone has their own specific blend of ingredients and proportions that they think works. And many chefs, myself included, have various blends for different uses. This is my go-to curry powder— the one I keep on hand all the time to add flavor and fabulousness to anything and everything.

6 cardamom pods
one 2-inch piece cinnamon,
    preferably Saigon
6 allspice berries
4 cloves

¼ cup coriander seeds
2 tablespoons cumin seeds
¼ cup ground turmeric
2 tablespoons white peppercorns
2 tablespoons kosher salt

**1** In a large dry sauté pan over medium heat, lightly toast the cardamom pods, cinnamon, allspice berries, cloves, coriander seeds and cumin seeds, starting with the largest spice first and gradually adding the others in order of decreasing size. Continue cooking, shaking the pan occasionally, until they're all aromatic, 3 to 4 minutes total. Add the ground turmeric to the pan and cook for another 15 to 20 seconds. Let all the spices cool completely (if the spices are still warm when ground the essential oils will stick to the inside of the grinder).

**2** Grind the toasted spices with the peppercorns and salt in a spice grinder until very fine. Keep in an airtight container for up to 3 months, or until ready to use.

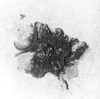

Charred Beef Lettuce Wraps with Pickled Carrots

# Crudo of Hamachi with Yuzu Vinaigrette

Oysters with Pineapple and Seaweed Mignonette

## Homemade Jarred Beet Salad with Sriracha

Tuna Tapanade with Green Olives and Celery

## Chilled Buckwheat Noodles with Hot-Sour Tamarind Broth

## Tangy Asian Shallots

Wok-Charred Napa Cabbage Kimchi Style

# Sweet and Sour Pickles

Tamarind Amaretto Sour

## Thai Basil and Cumin Lemonade

# Sour

# Sour | Lost and Found

**Ballplayers have slumps. Writers have blocks.** I don't know the name for what chefs experience when their creative juices slow down, but I know how it feels: totally frustrating, exhausting, and debilitating. You feel like something has been stolen from you—and you don't know where to begin looking to get it back.

A few years ago I was consulting for a bunch of hot restaurants, helping them develop new, edgy dishes when it happened. One day I suddenly felt completely empty. Whenever I tried to come up with something new, my brain went blank. I felt like my pulse was gone, like I was flat-lining. I kept searching for some flicker of inspiration, but it just wouldn't come. People say it happens, but it had never happed to me before. At first I sort of panicked; like a swimmer caught in a strong current, the more I struggled forward the farther out to sea I was pulled.

Week after week, day after day—still there was nothing. I knew I needed some clarity, something to brighten the darkness. Sunday came and I went to church. My church is in a preschool gym. It's very simple: metal folding chairs, children's drawings on the wall, and those squishy mats on the floor. Sitting there under the fluorescent lights I felt like I was back in school myself—when my mind was totally uncluttered and I was carefree. This whole experience of feeling so numb—like there was a dam inside holding everything back—began to evaporate. For the first time in weeks I felt all the tension and anxiety leave my body, my limbs relaxed and my mind quieted. I sat there, letting the sounds of the music float through my head, and all of a sudden I felt a surge of creativity, a waterfall of ideas streamed into my brain.

Fully composed dishes appeared in my mind's eye—every ingredient, every detail down to the last garnish. I was holding a yellow pamphlet from that morning's service and there were cans with pens strewn around the room—I frantically reached for a pen and began to write the ideas down as fast as possible, but I could barely keep up: beet tapioca caviar, curried shallot fondue with roasted chicken, slow-poached cod with chorizo purée and pistachio froth, pink peppercorn with white chocolate broth and chocolate dumplings, Gala apple soup with grated Roquefort and endive . . . As each one appeared on the paper I could visualize the final dish as though I'd made it hundreds of times before—I could almost taste it.

When I finished writing it all down I felt like a kid on the night before Christmas; I didn't even want to go to sleep. I was so jacked up with anticipation that I got to work early, with energy like I'd never had before. As soon as I had on my whites I grabbed my knife and started prepping. My sous chef Ricky was with me, and I told him what happened. I think at first he must have thought I was nuts, the chef saved by divine intervention! But once he heard my recipes he smiled and we just dove in and started cooking. I didn't even have to think about it; I cooked each of these new dishes like they had been in my repertoire for years. When I finally finished and tasted everything, I literally dropped my knife and fork. Ricky and I just looked at each other, then at the food, then back up at each other. I was in disbelief. Where had this come from? What had just happened? After such a dry spell I'd been graced with this abundance of creativity—and all of it, just perfectly conceived and executed as if by magic. I still don't know where it all came from, but I was thankful it did.

# Charred Beef Lettuce Wraps
## with Pickled Carrots

Serves: 4    Time: About 2½ hours    Flavors: Sour/Herbaceous/Sweet

When I have friends over this is one of my go-to dishes. It's interactive and fun. You can jazz it up with whatever herbs you fancy—I personally love the combination of Thai basil, mint, and cilantro. Sometimes I even add a bit of dill. And as anyone who knows me knows, I love anything you can eat with your hands. It's just so casual and sexy.

Pickled Carrots
1 cup seasoned rice wine vinegar
3 tablespoons sugar
2 large carrots, peeled

¼ cup light soy sauce
2 tablespoons toasted sesame oil
3 tablespoons gochujang paste
  (see Box, page 70)

2 tablespoons sugar
½ pound skirt steak
1 teaspoon kosher salt
fresh cilantro leaves
fresh mint leaves
fresh Thai basil leaves
1 head Bibb lettuce, leaves separated

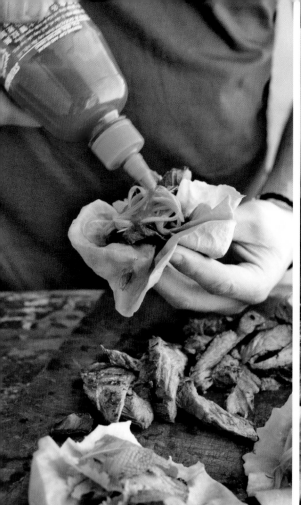

**1** First make the Pickled Carrots: In a medium bowl, combine the vinegar and sugar and stir until the sugar is completely dissolved. Shred the carrots using a mandoline, box shredder, or a food processor. Add the carrots to the vinegar mixture, transfer to the fridge, and let marinate for at least 2 hours or up to 24 hours.

**2** Meanwhile, in a large, shallow dish, combine the soy sauce, sesame oil, gochujang paste, and sugar and stir until the sugar dissolves. Pat the skirt steak dry with paper towels, season with the salt, and place the meat in the marinade. Let sit for 1 hour at room temperature.

**3** Heat a grill to high or a grill pan over medium-high heat. Remove the meat from the marinade, and grill over high heat, turning once, until browned on the exterior but still pink on the inside, about 3 minutes total depending on the thickness of the steak. Transfer to a cutting board and let rest for a few minutes. Cut the steak into thin slices, about ¼ inch thick, against the grain.

**4** To serve, wrap a couple of slices of meat in a lettuce leaf along with a few leaves of cilantro, mint, and Thai basil and a spoonful of the Pickled Carrots—these can be straight out of the fridge or at room temperature.

# Crudo of Hamachi
## with Yuzu Vinaigrette

Serves: 4    Time: About 20 minutes    Flavors: Sour/Sweet/Herbaceous

A traditional crudo is all about the simplicity and freshness of the fish. In this dish, the combination of the tart Japanese yuzu and a peppery extra virgin olive oil boost the lean hamachi with a bit of fat and brightness. On top of that, the addition of fleur de sel, or "flower of the sea," extracts the oceanic essence of the fish while also adding a bit of texture, a slight crunch with each bite. This is a very feminine dish: it's soft, subtle, and sensual all at the same time.

½ pound sashimi-grade hamachi
3 tablespoons yuzu juice (see Box, page 23)
3 tablespoons lemon juice
3 tablespoons extra virgin olive oil

2 tablespoons sugar
fleur de sel or other high-quality salt
freshly ground black pepper
4 fresh Thai basil leaves, torn

1 Use fish tweezers or needlenose pliers to remove all the pin bones from the fish. Slice the fish into very thin slivers against the grain. Place the fish on a serving platter and transfer to the fridge to chill while you make the vinaigrette.

2 In a small bowl, combine the yuzu juice and lemon juice, olive oil, and sugar and mix until thoroughly blended.

3 To serve, sprinkle the fish with a bit of fleur de sel and black pepper, drizzle with the vinaigrette, and garnish with the Thai basil.

When you're making crudo or serving any fish raw, it's imperative that you use #1 Grade (sashimi-quality). You always want to buy the best-quality fish available for health reasons, but it also tends to ensure better flavor—they go hand in hand. Look for fish that doesn't smell fishy and that has a pinkish tone to it.

# Oysters with Pineapple and Seaweed Mignonette

Serves: 2 to 4    Time: About 15 minutes    Flavors: Sour/Sweet/Fragrant

Growing up I spent my summers in Wellfleet, Cape Cod. Some of my most memorable times were digging for clams and oysters on the shore. Back then all seven of us kids would fill buckets with shellfish to take home for dinner. Writing this recipe just brought me back to those amazing times. What's beautiful about this dish is that the sweetness of the pineapple rounds out the acidity of the vinegar while the juniper accentuates the fruit's floral notes. To top it off, the wakame—seaweed—enhances the natural essence-of-the-sea flavor of the oysters.

1 cup pineapple juice
½ cup seasoned rice wine vinegar
1 tablespoon wakame seaweed
  (see Box)
1 tablespoon sugar
1 tablespoon fish sauce

¼ teaspoon kosher salt
2 tablespoons minced shallots
4 juniper berries, finely chopped
12 Kumamoto, Malpeque, or other
  mild, sweet oysters, shucked

**1** Put the pineapple juice, vinegar, wakame, sugar, fish sauce, and salt in a blender and purée. Strain the mixture through a fine sieve into a small bowl and chill in the fridge for about 20 minutes.

**2** To serve, stir the shallots and chopped juniper berries into the mignonette. Place the shucked oysters on a large platter and drizzle with the mignonette.

Wakame is an edible seaweed that has an amazing sweet flavor and a kind of silky texture. You've probably had it at Japanese restaurants—it's often served along with cubes of tofu in miso soup. You can usually find it in Asian markets and some grocery stores (see page 15).

# Homemade Jarred Beet Salad
## with Sriracha

Serves: 4   Time: About 2 hours   Flavors: Sour/Earthy/Floral

This is basically a portable salad; think of it as a salad in a jar. It mixes warm fall spices with an earthy vegetable and serves it up in a fresh way. Try this with a bit of creamy goat cheese or some salty Parmesan. Grab a good French baguette, a nice Riesling, and you've got my idea of the perfect picnic.

| | |
|---|---|
| 1 pound red baby beets, tops removed | 1 cup water |
| 6 allspice berries | ¼ cup olive oil |
| 2 cloves | ½ cup seasoned rice wine vinegar |
| 1 tablespoon coriander seeds | ½ cup red wine vinegar |
| 1 fresh rosemary sprig | ¼ cup sugar |
| 2 fresh thyme sprigs | 3 tablespoons Sriracha sauce |
| ½ teaspoon kosher salt | |

**1** Preheat the oven to 400°F. Put the beets, allspice berries, cloves, coriander seeds, rosemary, thyme, and salt in a roasting pan with the water and oil. Cover the pan with aluminum foil, place in the oven, and roast for about 45 minutes, until the beets are fork tender. Remove the beets from the oven and strain them from the cooking liquid, transferring the liquid to a bowl and setting it aside.

**2** When the beets are cool enough to handle, remove the skin (you may want to use paper towels so you don't stain your hands), cut them in quarters, and chill in the refrigerator for about 20 minutes.

**3** Meanwhile, add the rice wine vinegar, red wine vinegar, sugar, and Sriracha sauce to the reserved cooking liquid. Spoon the beets and marinade into jars and serve immediately, or refrigerate for up to a week.

# Tuna Tapenade
## with Green Olives and Celery

Serves: 4   Time: About 15 minutes   Flavors: Sour/Spicy/Salty

When I was working in the South of France, the other chefs and I would drive to Italy, just over the border, to go to the market for fresh tuna. The fishmonger would literally cut off a slab of fish right there in front of us. Then we'd whip it up with a fresh tapenade later that afternoon. It was utter simplicity, and in my opinion, it captured the essence of the Cote d'Azur. I've added to that original dish a bit over the years, and I love to serve my slightly tweaked version spooned onto grilled ciabatta with a drizzle of beautiful olive oil, wrapped in lettuce leaves, or just as a salad all by itself.

½ pound finely chopped sashimi-grade tuna
1 teaspoon kosher salt
¼ cup olive oil
½ red Thai chile, chopped

1 teaspoon fresh thyme leaves
6 chopped green Cerignola olives
3 tablespoons finely chopped celery, plus celery leaves for garnish

1 Put the tuna, salt, olive oil, chile, and thyme in a standing mixer with the paddle attachment or a food processor, and whip until the mixture is creamy.

2 To serve, transfer the tuna mixture to a plate and garnish with the olives, celery, and celery leaves.

# Chilled Buckwheat Noodles
## with Hot-Sour Tamarind Broth

Serves: 4   Time: About 45 minutes   Flavors: Sour/Sweet/Salty

One of my favorite things to do on a free afternoon is head to Flushing, Queens, for chilled Korean noodles. But I also love hitting Chinatown for hot and sour soup. So in this recipe I brought the best of both of these Asian worlds together. You get the toothsome tug of the buckwheat noodles combined with the sourness of the tamarind, the sweetness of the pineapple, and the hotness of the gochujang paste.

kosher salt
8 ounces buckwheat noodles
1 tablespoon grapeseed oil
½ cup tamarind paste
2 cups pineapple juice
1 cup orange juice
¼ cup lime juice

¼ cup light soy sauce
3 tablespoons gochujang paste
  (see Box, page 70)
3 tablespoons Sriracha sauce
3 tablespoons sugar
2 scallions, sliced on the diagonal

1 Bring a large pot of salted water to a boil over high heat. Add the buckwheat noodles and cook until just done—they should still have a bit of a bite to them—about 4 minutes. Drain the noodles in a colander, transfer to a bowl, toss with the oil to prevent sticking, and transfer to the fridge until ready to use.

2 In a large saucepan over medium-high heat, combine the tamarind paste, pineapple juice, orange juice, lime juice, soy sauce, gochujang paste, Sriracha sauce, sugar, and 1 teaspoon salt. Bring to a boil, stirring to thoroughly combine all the ingredients, and remove from the heat. Transfer the mixture to a blender and purée until smooth. Refrigerate until chilled, about 30 minutes.

3 To serve, place the noodles in soup bowls, pour the chilled broth over the top, and garnish with a few slices of scallion.

# Tangy Asian
## Shallots

Makes: About 2 cups    Time: About 1½ hours    Flavors: Sour/Sweet/Spicy

This is the epitome of what a condiment should be. You get the crunch of the shallots, the bite of the ginger, and the heat of the chile. I'd serve these with almost anything—burgers, steak, scrambled eggs, fried rice, salad, sandwiches, well, like I said, pretty much anything. I've even been known to stand over the sink and eat them straight.

2 cups seasoned rice wine vinegar
3 tablespoons olive oil
½ cup sugar
1 red Thai chile, minced

1 tablespoons grated ginger
2 cups thinly sliced shallots
    (8 to 10 shallots)

**1** In a medium bowl, combine the vinegar, oil, sugar, chile, and ginger, and stir until the sugar is dissolved. Add the shallots and refrigerate for at least 1 hour. Serve when chilled, or transfer to an airtight container and keep for up to 3 months in the fridge.

# Wok-Charred Napa Cabbage
## Kimchi Style

**Serves: 4   Time: About 15 minutes   Flavors: Sour/Salty/Spicy**

Kimchi, a Korean staple, is fermented cabbage that's been salted and marinated in chile paste (in many homes they actually bury it underground to moderate the temperature and help with the preservation process). My version is basically a quick wok-fried kimchi—an unorthodox, though yummy take on the traditional style. The key here is to extract the dragon's breath flavor from the wok—it adds a totally new dimension. Serve this with fried rice.

**1 pound Napa cabbage**
**3 tablespoons grapeseed oil**
**2 teaspoons coriander seeds, cracked**
**¼ cup thinly sliced red onion**
**¼ cup sambal (see Box)**
**3 tablespoons gochujang paste**
**(see Box, page 70)**

**¼ cup red wine vinegar**
**2 tablespoons fish sauce**
**1 teaspoon kosher salt**
**1 tablespoon toasted sesame oil**
**fresh cilantro leaves**

**1** Cut the cabbage into quarters lengthwise, then cut the quarters horizontally into large cubes.

**2** Put the oil in a large wok or sauté pan over medium heat. When the oil is hot, add the coriander seeds and toast until they pop, about 30 seconds. Increase the heat to high and add the cabbage. Continue to toss the cabbage in the oil until coated, then add the onions and cook for 1 minute more.

**3** Add the sambal, gochujang paste, vinegar, fish sauce, and salt and continue cooking, stirring frequently, until the cabbage is wilted but still crunchy on the inside, another 2 or 3 minutes. Transfer to a platter, drizzle with the sesame oil, toss, and serve garnished with cilantro leaves.

# Sweet and Sour
## Pickles

Serves: 4 to 6   Time:  About 1¼ hours   Flavors: Sour/Spicy/Salty

These pickles are like a journey through Asia; they're sweet, sour, salty, spicy, and acidic all at once. In the restaurant we make them in batches and keep them on hand to serve with grilled meats and fish, satay, and sandwiches—but they're great on their own as a little snack with cocktails (think Asian olives). For some reason people think pickling is complicated—these pickles do have a complex flavor, but they couldn't be simpler to make.

1 tablespoon mustard seeds
1½ cups seasoned rice wine vinegar
½ cup sugar
1 teaspoon kosher salt
½ teaspoon ground turmeric
¼ cup chopped fresh dill

1 Thai chile, split
1 cup cauliflower florets
2 tablespoons thinly sliced shallots
1 cup sliced carrots, sliced diagonally
    about ¼-inch thick

1 In a small dry sauté pan over low heat, lightly toast the mustard seeds until aromatic, 2 to 4 minutes.

2 In a large bowl, combine the vinegar, sugar, salt, turmeric, dill, chile, and toasted mustard seeds. Add the cauliflower, shallots, and carrots to the pickling liquid and marinate for about 1 hour at room temperature.

3 Divide the vegetables and pickling liquid evenly into airtight glass jars and use as desired. Refrigerated, these will hold indefinitely.

# Tamarind
## Amaretto Sour

**Serves: 4  Time: About 10 minutes  Flavors: Sour/Sweet/Nutty**

Traveling throughout Malaysia, specifically in Penang, I was aware of a dominant Indian influence, and it really captured my imagination. Walking around I was amazed to see tamarind pods, a classic Indian ingredient, right there in the trees! That experience inspired me to create this refreshingly tart, sweet, nutty, luscious drink. With a touch of candied ginger, this is an exotic journey in a glass.

4 allspice berries
1 cup amaretto
¼ cup tamarind paste
1 egg white
¼ cup Sprite

3 tablespoons lime juice
¼ cup agave nectar
2 tablespoons candied ginger
ice

**1** In a small dry sauté pan, toast the allspice berries over low heat for about 2 minutes, or until aromatic.

**2** Place the amaretto, tamarind paste, egg white, Sprite, lime juice, agave nectar, candied ginger, and toasted allspice berries in a shaker. Shake well, pour into highball glasses over ice, and serve.

# Thai Basil
## and Cumin Lemonade

**Serves: 4   Time: About 15 minutes   Flavors: Sour/Sweet/Herbaceous**

If my son ever decides to have a lemonade stand, I'd like to think I'd have some influence over his product. If so, this would be my suggestion for our collaborative effort: a refreshing, fragrant beverage suitable for all ages. Seriously, I'm pretty sure this is a get-rich-quick idea for a small business, so if you want to steal it and start a Thai Basil and Cumin Lemonade stand, by all means, go for it.

| | |
|---|---|
| 2 cups fresh lemon juice | 2 tablespoons sliced ginger |
| 1½ cups water | 2 teaspoons cumin seeds |
| 1½ cups sugar | ice |
| 2 fresh sprigs Thai basil, plus leaves | |

**1** In a large pitcher, combine the lemon juice, water, sugar, Thai basil, and ginger.

**2** Put the cumin seeds in a small dry sauté pan over low heat and toast until just aromatic, about 2 minutes. Immediately add the warm cumin seeds to infuse the lemonade with the cumin flavor and stir to dissolve the sugar. Refrigerate until fully chilled, about 30 minutes.

**3** To serve, mix again and pour over ice. Garnish with Thai basil leaves.

Crispy Spring Roll with Calamansi Duck Sauce

Taiwanese Tea Eggs

Far East Egg Salad

Crudo of Flounder with Seaweed Ponzu

Gochujang Glazed Beef

Vietnamese Shaken Beef Tartare

Slow-Braised Pork Belly with Pineapple and Kimchi

Soy-Steeped Chicken with Tea Leaves

Spiced Chicken Cutlets with Bonito Salt

Bombay Fish Tacos

Kai-Lan, Oyster Sauce, and Garlic Chips

"This is Hot" Chile Sauce

# Umami 6

# Umami | Tough Love

Every day as a kid I would sit in the playground with my Dukes of Hazzard lunchbox—Bo, Luke, Daisy, and that 1969 red Dodge Charger staring back at me—and wonder what I'd find inside. I wasn't raised like other kids when it came to a lot of things, and when it came to food things were especially strange. There were no peanut butter-and-jelly sandwiches for me, no ham and cheese, no Twinkies, and certainly no chips. No, my lunches were more likely to consist of pickled pigs' feet, olive loaf, or maybe a cow's tongue sandwich. As you can imagine, no one ever wanted to trade with me.

But then there was Friday, the best day of the week as far as I was concerned. Friday was Pizza Day in the school cafeteria. Of course I wasn't allowed to buy pizza like the other kids. However, my mother kept a tin in the top kitchen drawer for our milk money and each day I'd go in and get my quarters like I was supposed to, but then I'd save them up all week to buy a single precious slice on Friday. I still love pizza, and in fact when people ask me what my last meal on earth would be I always say "pepperoni pizza and kimchi." But back then pizza was my salvation.

It took years, but I grew to appreciate that those lunches I hated so much were actually a gift. They weren't fun for a kid, but they helped shape me, helped me become the chef I am today by providing me with something very special: an educated palate and an inherent desire for adventure and new experiences. Certainly I learned to taste anything (and clean my plate whether I wanted to or not), but I also learned how to get creative with food. I'd open up our cupboard praying just once to find a package of Oreos, but instead see those same Italian amaretti cookies my parents loved. So I'd eat those with a bowl of pickles. Little did I realize that this early exposure to unusual ingredients was teaching me to think creatively, and to rely on flavor combinations rather than just traditional ideas of what works together.

Also from those lunches that my mother sent me off with every day, I learned that to understand a cuisine you have to first understand the culture it comes from. You have to be open to other ways of doing things, to other ingredients, and to other less familiar tastes and flavors if you want to be truly creative in the kitchen. I've always liked to think of myself as a chef who has one foot in the past—who understands the traditions behind food—as well as one foot always moving toward the future, looking for new combinations and new dishes. My mother, with all her wacky ethnic foods and her resistance to Fig Newtons and Cheetos, gave me the ability to respect all different kinds of cuisine, the curiosity to want to understand why things are done the way they are, and the encouragement to discover how I can tweak them to make them new and fresh at the same time. It's a gift I wouldn't trade for anything in the world. Thanks, Mom.

# Crispy Spring Roll
# with Calamansi Duck Sauce

Serves: 12   Time: About 1½ hours   Flavors: Umami/Sweet/Sour

When I was in Hong Kong, working in a Cantonese-style dim sum kitchen, I learned this technique for brushing spring roll wrappers with egg yolk. The spring rolls we made there were crisp and the filling stayed moist. I've adopted this technique because it allows all of the various elements of the dish to come through—the beauty of the crisp exterior and the tender, flavorful, and colorful interior. I finish the spring rolls with my own version of duck sauce—a combination of Japanese and Southeast Asian flavors that come together to heighten the whole experience.

¼ cup grapeseed oil, plus more
   for frying
2 tablespoons grated ginger
2 tablespoons minced garlic
1 pound ground chicken
2 cups shredded green cabbage
1 cup shredded carrot
2 cups stemmed and chopped shiitake
   mushrooms
2 tablespoons cornstarch
3 tablespoons water
1 cup shredded jicama
½ pound medium shrimp (16/20),
   peeled, deveined, and cut into
   large chunks
¼ cup chopped fresh cilantro
1 tablespoon kosher salt,
   plus more as needed

½ cup light soy sauce
3 tablespoons toasted sesame oil
24 spring roll wrappers
6 egg yolks

Calamansi Duck Sauce
3 tablespoons grapeseed oil
1 cup chopped shallots
2 cups calamansi juice (see Box,
   page 57) or 1 cup lemon and
   1 cup orange juice combined
1 cup candied ginger
¼ cup sugar
2 tablespoons minced garlic
2 tablespoons ground turmeric
2 tablespoons Togarashi Salt (page 53)
1 teaspoon kosher salt

1 Put the ¼ cup oil in a large saucepan over medium-high heat. When the oil is hot, add the ginger and garlic and cook until just aromatic, 1 to 2 minutes. Increase the heat to high, add the chicken, and cook for another 2 to 3 minutes, until about halfway done. Add the cabbage, carrots, and mushrooms and cook for 5 minutes.

2 Meanwhile, combine the cornstarch and water in a small bowl and mix well to make a smooth slurry. Avoid any lumps.

3 When the vegetables have wilted, add the jicama, shrimp, cilantro, 1 tablespoon salt, and soy sauce and stir continuously to deglaze the pan. Once the mixture is well combined and the soy sauce simmers, add the slurry to the pan, and continue stirring for 3 minutes, or until the liquid appears glossy. Remove the pan from the heat, add the sesame oil, toss to combine, transfer to a large bowl, and chill in the fridge until cool enough to handle, about 15 minutes.

4 Meanwhile, make the Calamansi Duck Sauce: Put the oil in a large saucepan over medium heat. When the oil is hot, add the shallots and cook until just soft, 3 to 5 minutes. Add the calamansi juice, candied ginger, sugar, garlic, turmeric,

Togarashi Salt, and kosher salt and cook for another 15 minutes. Transfer to a blender and purée until smooth. Set aside to come to room temperature.

**5** To assemble the spring rolls, lay a spring roll wrapper on a clean work surface with the corners pointing east to west. Whisk the egg yolks together in a small bowl until thoroughly combined. Brush the entire surface of the wrapper with the egg yolk (this helps ensure that when you fry the spring rolls the liquid from the filling doesn't soften the wrapper). Spoon about 3 tablespoons of the filling onto the back third of the wrapper closest to you. Fold the east and west corners in over the filling, then tightly roll the wrapper up.

**6** Pour enough oil into a large pot to come about 3 inches up the sides. Turn the heat to high and bring to 325°F, as measured by a deep-fry or candy thermometer. Meanwhile, line a sheet pan with paper towels and put it by the stove to hold the spring rolls as they come out of the oil.

**7** When the oil is ready, add the spring rolls to the pot. When they are golden and crisp, about 2 minutes, use a slotted spoon to carefully transfer them to the prepared sheet pan to drain any excess oil. While they're still hot, sprinkle the rolls lightly with salt and serve with the Calamansi Duck Sauce.

# Taiwanese
## Tea Eggs

**Makes: 12   Time:  About 1 hour   Flavors: Umami/Salty/Smoky**

These are the hippest hard-boiled eggs you'll ever have. You cook them with smoky bacon in a soy broth (which you can drink), so they're infused with robust flavors. They make a killer Far East Egg Salad (see opposite), are an amazing complement to noodles or rice, or work beautifully on their own as a really sexy side. Dish up a little shot of the broth to serve with them and you will seriously impress your dinner guests.

| | |
|---|---|
| 12 large eggs | 1 teaspoon black peppercorns |
| 4 ounces smoked bacon | ¼ cup light soy sauce |
| 4 cardamom pods | fresh cilantro leaves |
| 2 star anise | chopped scallions |

**1** Bring a large pot of water to a boil. Add the eggs and cook for 7 minutes at a rolling boil. Drain, run the eggs under cold water, and remove the shells. Set aside.

**2** In the same pot, cook the bacon over medium heat until the fat has rendered. Add the cardamom and star anise to the pot and cook for about 1 minute, until just fragrant. Then add the peppercorns and continue cooking until the spices release their aromatic oils, about 2 minutes total.

**3** Add 4 cups of water to the pot along with the soy sauce and reserved eggs. Bring to a boil, reduce the heat, and continue to cook at a low simmer for 30 minutes. Remove the eggs from the cooking liquid, strain the liquid through a fine-mesh sieve into a large bowl, and add the eggs back in.

**4** To serve, put one egg in a serving bowl with a cup or so of broth and garnish with the cilantro and scallions. Or keep refrigerated for up to 2 weeks.

# Far East
## Egg Salad

**Serves: 4   Time: About 20 minutes   Flavors: Umami/Earthy/Herbaceous**

This is an Asian take on the classic American egg salad. It can be served as a small side salad, on top of bitter greens, as filling for lettuce wraps, or even lightly puréed and dished up with chips for dipping. If you want to go old school, just spread it on rye or seven-grain bread for awesome egg salad sandwiches.

**8 Taiwanese Eggs (see opposite)**
**½ cup mayonnaise**
**2 tablespoons Sriracha sauce**
**¼ cup diced celery**
**¼ cup diced red onion**

**1 teaspoon chopped fresh thyme**
**3 tablespoons chopped fresh cilantro**
**3 tablespoons thinly sliced scallion**
**2 tablespoons seasoned rice wine vinegar**

**1** Roughly chop the Taiwanese Eggs and place them in a large bowl with the mayonnaise, Sriracha sauce, celery, onion, thyme, cilantro, scallion, and vinegar. Mix gently to avoid breaking the eggs up too much. Serve as desired.

# Crudo of Flounder
## with Seaweed Ponzu

Serves: 4   Time: About 30 minutes   Flavors: Umami/Salty/Sweet

Flounder is a very mild, sweet fish. Here I dress the flounder with a seaweed ponzu to extract its natural sweetness and to balance it out with light salty tones. A touch of pear in the sauce accentuates the delicate taste of the fish and adds a refreshing, crisp, cleansing flavor. It's an insanely simple dish to pull together, but the flavors are truly complex.

2 cups water
½ cup light soy sauce
¼ cup sugar
3 tablespoons yuzu juice (see Box, page 23) or lemon juice
2 tablespoons wakame seaweed
2 teaspoons grated ginger

3 tablespoons grated Asian or Bosc pear
8 ounces flounder, skin removed
¼ teaspoon fleur de sel or other high-quality salt
3 tablespoons olive oil
3 tablespoons chopped fresh cilantro

1 Combine the water, soy sauce, sugar, yuzu juice, wakame, ginger, and pear in a blender and purée until smooth. Strain through a fine-mesh sieve and chill in the fridge for 15 to 20 minutes.

2 Meanwhile, thinly slice the flounder against the grain into ¼-inch pieces. Place the fish on a serving dish, season with the fleur de sel, and drizzle with the olive oil. To serve, drizzle the chilled ponzu over the flounder and garnish with the cilantro.

# Gochujang
## Glazed Beef

**Serves: 4   Time: About 1 hour   Flavors: Umami/Spicy/Sweet**

Walking on the streets of Bangkok a few years ago, I found myself following the aromas of char-grilled meat coming from the hawker stands; the chile-scented air would lure me along for hours at a time. Inspired by these amazing scents and totally obsessed with gochujang paste, I came up with this delicious satay.

¼ cup gochujang paste (see Box, page 70)
2 tablespoons seasoned rice wine vinegar
3 tablespoons Worcestershire sauce

2 tablespoons toasted sesame oil
¼ cup sugar
1 teaspoon kosher salt
½ pound beef chuck, cut into ¼-inch-thick rectangular pieces

**1** If using wooden skewers, soak in water for at least 10 minutes to avoid splintering.

**2** Combine the gochujang paste, vinegar, Worcestershire sauce, sesame oil, sugar, and salt in a large, wide dish and mix until the sugar is dissolved. Add the beef and let stand at room temperature for 30 minutes.

**3** Heat a grill to high or a grill pan over medium-high heat. Thread the meat onto skewers. Cook the beef for 1 minute per side, or until nicely browned on the exterior but still pink in the middle. Serve immediately.

# Vietnamese Shaken
## Beef Tartare

**Serves: 4**   **Time: About 20 minutes**   **Flavors: Umami/Spicy/Herbaceous**

Shaken beef is a traditional Vietnamese dish, typically "shaken" in a wok. Tartare is a classic French dish—chopped beef served raw. I've fused these two greats to come up with something I think you'll find very cool—not to mention absolutely delicious.

1 pound sirloin beef
2 tablespoons grapeseed oil
3 tablespoons olive oil
1 tablespoon gochujang paste
  (see Box, page 70)
1 tablespoon lime juice
2 tablespoons seasoned rice wine
vinegar

2 tablespoons fish sauce
1 tablespoon Sriracha sauce
2 teaspoons grated ginger
1½ teaspoons kosher salt
1 teaspoon sugar
1 tablespoon sesame seeds, toasted
2 tablespoons chopped fresh mint

**1** Mince the beef and set aside. Place a large sauté pan over high heat. When the pan is piping hot, remove it from the heat, add the grapeseed oil, swirl to coat the bottom of the pan, add the meat, and toss quickly until just coated in the oil (the beef will still be raw, but "shaken"). Transfer the meat to a bowl and immediately place in the fridge.

**2** In a separate bowl, combine the olive oil, gochujang paste, lime juice, vinegar, fish sauce, Sriracha sauce, ginger, salt, and sugar; mix until the sugar is dissolved. Add the chilled beef, sesame seeds, and mint. Toss gently to combine and serve.

# Slow-Braised Pork Belly
## with Pineapple and Kimchi

Serves: 4   Time: About 4 hours   Flavors: Umami/Sweet/Spicy

The flavors in this dish are very clear and distinct: the umami of the pork belly, the sweet of the pineapple, and the spice of the kimchi. What I love here is that the combo of the sweetness and the acidity of the pineapple cleanses and refreshes the palate and the kimchi offers up beautiful textural stimulation.

1 pound pork belly
2 cups chicken stock
2 cups water
½ cup light soy sauce
2 cups minced pineapple, plus 2 cups
  pineapple scraps (skin is fine too)
one 2-inch piece ginger, thickly sliced

1 lemongrass stalk, smashed
1 teaspoon kosher salt
1 cup minced kimchi
3 tablespoons sugar
2 tablespoons olive oil
1 tablespoon chopped fresh cilantro

**1** Preheat the oven to 300°F.

**2** Put a large roasting pan over medium-high heat. Add the pork belly, fat-side down, and sear until deeply browned, about 10 minutes. Add the chicken stock, water, soy sauce, pineapple scraps, ginger, lemongrass, and salt and bring to a boil, then reduce to a simmer. Cover the pan with aluminum foil and place in the oven for 2½ to 3 hours, until fork tender.

**3** Meanwhile, combine the 2 cups diced pineapple and kimchi in a medium bowl. Add the sugar, olive oil, and cilantro, stir well, and chill until ready to serve.

**4** When the pork is done, remove it from the liquid. Carefully strain the braising liquid through a fine-mesh sieve and add it back to the pan. Put the pan over medium-high heat and reduce, stirring frequently, until it's the consistency of light cream and just coats the back of spoon, about 10 minutes.

**5** Cut the pork into 2-inch-square cubes. To serve, place the pork on a large platter, drizzle with the reduced braising liquid, and top with spoonfuls of the pineapple-kimchi mixture.

# Soy-Steeped Chicken
## with Tea Leaves

Serves: 8   Time: About 1 hour   Flavors: Umami/Earthy/Fragrant

I learned how to make this chicken from an Amah in Hong Kong, a woman who had cooked for the family I was visiting for over fifty years. In the version she taught me, the chicken was poached on the bone for about an hour—usually using an older chicken for an intense, robust flavor. I wanted to update both the flavor and the process a bit, so in my version I ditch the bone and steep the chicken in flavorful liquid (just like you would with tea). This allows the bird to absorb flavor and extracts its natural sweetness while keeping the meat tender and succulent.

4 cups water
1½ cups light soy sauce
1 cup sugar
3 tablespoons Oolong tea leaves
1 teaspoon kosher salt

one 2-inch piece ginger
2 pounds boneless chicken
   breast, skin on
1 tablespoon chopped fresh
   cilantro

**1** Put the water, soy sauce, sugar, tea leaves, salt, and ginger in a large saucepan over medium-high heat and bring to a boil. Reduce the heat to a simmer and cook for 20 minutes. Reduce the heat to low, add the chicken, and cook for another 15 minutes. Remove the pan from the heat and let the chicken cool in the liquid.

**2** When the liquid reaches room temperature, use a slotted spoon to remove the chicken from the cooking liquid and slice against the grain. Strain the cooking liquid and pour over the chicken to serve. Garnish with the cilantro.

# Spiced Chicken Cutlets
# with Bonito Salt

Serves: 4   Time: About 30 minutes   Flavors: Umami/Smoky/Salty

I like to say this recipe is like Marco Polo leaving Italy for Central Asia and somehow ending up with a layover in Japan. It brings a classic Tuscan preparation together with some truly exotic flavors, and it's totally awesome—not to mention easy.

Bonito Salt
½ ounce bonito flakes
1½ tablespoons kosher salt

1 tablespoon coriander seeds
1 tablespoon cumin seeds
1 tablespoon kosher salt
4 boneless, skinless chicken breasts

½ cup all-purpose flour
2 tablespoons dried oregano
2 large eggs
2 cups panko breadcrumbs
3 tablespoons grapeseed oil
1 lemon, quartered

1 First make the Bonito Salt: Put the bonito shavings and salt in a spice grinder and blend until fine; set aside.

2 In a small skillet over low heat, lightly toast the coriander and cumin seeds until aromatic, 2 to 4 minutes. Cool to room temperature and blend to a fine powder in a spice grinder. Add the salt and continue to blend until well combined; set aside.

3 Lay the chicken breasts flat on a work surface. Using a sharp knife, butterfly each breast by cutting horizontally down the cutlet without cutting all the way through the meat. Season each of the breasts with about 1 tablespoon of the spice mixture.

4 Combine the flour and oregano in a low, wide dish. Crack the eggs into another low, wide dish and whisk them well. Put the breadcrumbs in a third dish. Dredge the cutlets in the flour, shaking off any excess, then dip them in the eggs, and then dredge them in the breadcrumbs, pressing the crumbs on gently if necessary.

5 Put the oil in a large sauté pan over medium-high heat and add the cutlets (work in batches if necessary to avoid crowding the pan). Cook until golden brown on one side, then repeat with the second side. Continue cooking until the meat is cooked through, 6 to 8 minutes total. Transfer to paper towels to drain any excess oil.

6 Season the cutlets with the Bonito Salt and serve with a slice of lemon.

Bonito flakes come from dried fish and are most commonly used in Japanese cooking. They add a smoky, oceanic flavor to this salt that I just love. You can find bonito flakes in most Asian markets.

# Bombay
## Fish Tacos

Serves: 4   Time: About 1 hour   Flavors: Umami/Salty/Herbaceous

I have this amazing idea for a restaurant: an Asian taquería. A combination of Mexican dishes using Asian ingredients seems like a no-brainer to me. So I came up with these fish tacos—great guacamole, good-quality corn tortillas, and Asian-spiced fish—what's not to love? I add a hefty bit of dill to brighten it up and then douse it with Sriracha for some heat . . . delicioso!

½ tablespoon cumin seeds
1 tablespoon coriander seeds
1 tablespoon ground turmeric
8 ounces red snapper or any lean
   white fish
½ teaspoon kosher salt
6 tablespoons fish sauce
2 tablespoons grapeseed oil
8 corn tortillas
2 cups shredded iceberg lettuce
fresh dill

Guacamole
2 avocados
3 tablespoons minced jalapeño chile
3 tablespoons minced red onion
¼ cup lime juice
2 tablespoons olive oil
3 tablespoons fresh cilantro leaves
about 1 teaspoon kosher salt

**1** In a small sauté pan over medium heat, lightly toast the cumin and coriander seeds and the turmeric until the essential oils are extracted. Start with the larger seeds first and add the turmeric last. Continue cooking, shaking the pan occasionally, until they're aromatic, 2 to 3 minutes total. Let cool completely, then grind the spices in a spice grinder until very fine.

**2** Cut the fish into rectangles, about the size of your finger, and put them on a large platter in a single layer. Coat the fish thoroughly in the spice rub, sprinkle with the salt, and drizzle with the fish sauce. Cover with plastic wrap and marinate at room temperature for 30 minutes.

**3** Meanwhile, make the guacamole: Cut the avocados in half, remove the pits, scoop out the flesh, and cut into large chunks. Put half in a medium bowl and use the back of a fork to mash it until a paste forms. Add the jalapeño, onion, lime juice, oil, and cilantro and stir to combine. Add the remaining avocado half, mix gently, and season with salt as needed. Set aside.

**4** In a large sauté pan, heat the oil over medium-high heat. When it's hot, add the fish, in batches if necessary, and cook until caramelized on all sides, 1 to 2 minutes total. Transfer to a sheet pan and set aside.

**5** Wrap the tortillas in a damp kitchen towel and steam in the microwave until soft, about 1 minute or less. Using tongs, carefully flash each tortilla over a burner, turning once, to release the corn flavor.

**6** To serve, mound ¼ cup of lettuce on top of each tortilla, add a generous dollop of guacamole, and top with a piece of fish. Garnish each with a large piece of dill.

# Kai-Lan, Oyster Sauce, and Garlic Chips

**Serves: 4   Time: About 20 minutes   Flavors: Umami/Salty/Spicy**

There's something beautiful about how simple this dish is to make and how totally layered the flavors are. If I ever throw an Asian-inspired Thanksgiving I'm serving this: Think how fabulous the crunchy texture of the kai-lan (Chinese broccoli) would be served with a tender Southeast Asian–flavored turkey.

| | |
|---|---|
| 2 tablespoons grapeseed oil | 2 tablespoons Worcestershire sauce |
| 1 tablespoon thinly sliced garlic | 1 red Thai chile |
| 1 tablespoon grated ginger | 1 tablespoon red wine vinegar or |
| 1 pound kai-lan, whole (see Box) |   black vinegar |
| 3 tablespoons water | 3 tablespoons sugar |
| 3 tablespoons oyster sauce | 2 tablespoons toasted sesame oil |

**1** Add the oil to a wok or large sauté pan placed over medium-high heat. When the oil is hot, add the garlic and cook, stirring frequently, until it's golden brown, 2 to 3 minutes. Use a slotted spoon to transfer the garlic to paper towels to drain.

**2** Add the ginger to the garlic oil and cook for 30 seconds, or until just aromatic; add the kai-lan, increase the heat to high, and cook for 1 minute, then add the water, oyster sauce, Worcestershire sauce, chile, vinegar, and sugar and cook until the kai-lan is wilted and glazed with the sauce, about 2 minutes more.

**3** To serve, transfer the kai-lan to a large plate, drizzle with the sesame oil, and scatter the garlic chips over the top.

Kai-lan, or Chinese broccoli, is a leafy vegetable that's similar in flavor to broccoli but slightly more bitter. The large leaves are perfect for stir-frying, as they wilt but still hold their structure. You can find kai-lan in Chinatown, but if you can't find it, regular broccoli or broccolini can be used for a similar flavor.

# "This Is Hot" Chile Sauce

**Makes: About 1 cup   Time: 30 minutes   Flavors: Umami/Spicy/Earthy**

I often add cloves to my dishes because they numb the palate a bit and help suppress more intense spices, allowing them to seep in gradually and giving your brain a chance to really process the different flavors. What I love about this recipe is that there are four different dimensions of spice here: You get the warmth of the fall spices (the cloves and allspice), the smokiness of the chipotle, the brighter more direct spice notes from the fresh chiles, and finally the fermented and aged spice notes from the gochujang paste. Serve this as a condiment with burgers or tacos, or add a few drops to any caramel sauce (yes, I'm serious) for a kick of heat.

6 allspice berries
4 cloves
1 teaspoon kosher salt
¼ cup gochujang paste (see Box,
  page 70)
¼ cup chipotle chiles in adobo sauce

2 red Thai chiles
¼ cup sugar
½ cup water
1 tablespoon seasoned rice wine
  vinegar

**1** In a medium dry sauté pan over low heat, lightly toast the allspice berries and cloves until just aromatic, about 2 minutes. Cool completely, then grind the allspice and cloves with the salt in a spice grinder until fine.

**2** Combine the gochujang paste, chipotles, Thai chiles, sugar, water, vinegar, and ground spices in a small saucepan over medium heat and cook for 15 minutes, or until the mixture reaches the consistency of light syrup. Transfer to a blender and purée until smooth. Serve immediately or store in an airtight container in the fridge for up to 3 months.

Pineapple and Celery Salad with Sambal

Spiced Watermelon Salad with Aleppo Pepper

# Hot and Sour Chicken Fling

Chicken Hot Dogs with Sweet and Sourkraut

## Franco-Vietnamese Lobster Rolls with Crispy Shallots

Blackened Swordfish with Spiced Pepper Relish

# Spiced Shrimp Po' Boy

## Red Snapper a la Chaca

Wok-Charred Baby Bok Choy with Finger Chiles

# Piri Piri Chile Relish

## Curried Pots de Creme

Spiced Ketchup

Jalapeño and Lemongrass     Vinaigrette

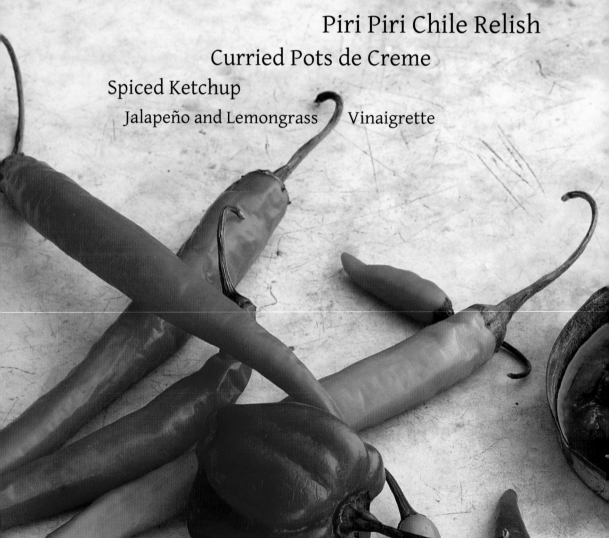

# Spicy 7

# Spicy | Homage to Alain Ducasse

**Life is so amazing—you set yourself on a path,** you think you know exactly where you're going, where you want to end up. Then there's an unexpected curve in the road. Destiny, fate, whatever you want it call it, some larger force takes over and you just have to embrace it. Here's how it went down for me.

It's three months since the opening of my first restaurant, Yumcha, and I've never worked this hard in my life. I'm exhilarated by what my team and I have built and the only hours I know are 6 a.m. and 2 a.m.—when I get up and when I leave the restaurant. It's Sunday and I'm looking forward to my first half day off since opening. My game plan is to work half a shift and let my sous chefs cover the rest.

Yumcha was designed like a sushi bar with customers sitting at a black-lacquer counter facing a pristine open kitchen. I'm standing behind the counter totally focused on my prep when one of my chefs nudges me and says that Alain Ducasse, the world-famous French chef, has just walked in. I stop, I look up, I can't wrap my head around this. All my life I have aspired to be like Ducasse, he's my idol, and here he is in my tiny neighborhood restaurant. I take a deep breath and think to myself, "Angelo, this is awesome. This is everything you've wanted. Go for it—step up to the plate." With another very deep breath, I lean across the counter and say simply, "Mr. Ducasse, welcome, it would be an honor to cook for you."

This salad is a beautiful contrast of textures and colors, a mind-blowing combo of flavors.

Now the game is on and I'm totally in my zone; all I can hear is the chef inside me running through ingredients, ticking off dishes, pulling it all together. I start by serving him a peanut noodle salad topped with lime sorbet, a killer dish served in a bowl with a clear plastic plate on top laden with garnishes. I place the bowl in front of him and a waiter comes over and sweeps a knife across the plate, brushing all the garnishes into the bowl. This salad is a beautiful contrast of textures and colors, a mind-blowing combo of flavors. It's edgy and unorthodox—not at all what you would call traditional—but I'm hoping he'll get a kick out of it.

As Ducasse begins to eat I start preparing his next dish, but I'm also trying to gauge his feelings about the food. The greatest—and worst—thing about an open kitchen is you can see people's reactions. I keep thinking he's not going to like it; it's too modern, the Asian flavors won't work for him. While I'm preparing the next course—a French-inspired, Asian-infused dish of chile frog legs with crispy ginger garlic served with a pineapple shooter—the voice inside my head starts in, "Angelo, how can you serve such a prestigious chef a shooter? This isn't happy hour."

I'm deep in the middle of torturing myself, when I look up to see him flipping through a little book and making notes. I turn to Lon, my sous chef, and whisper in panic, "What the hell is he writing down?" while preparing the third course—a slow-poached halibut served in a Chinese sausage broth with a fermented black bean crust and agar noodles. This is it: the telltale dish. I place the bowl in front of him and the waiter pours the broth over the noodles—the hot broth gently melting the noodles and perfuming the liquid as a savory vapor rises up from the bowl. All of us turn to watch for his reaction. He tastes it and stands up. We're all thinking he's going to walk out—it's over—our hearts all drop in unison. Instead, he turns, bows his head slightly, and blows me a kiss. My heart leaps, or drops again, I don't know exactly which, but then I just continue cooking. After all, I still have a full restaurant to run.

I thought this would be the end of my Alain Ducasse story, but the next day I receive a cookbook and a thank-you letter from him. Then a month later I receive an e-mail saying that he wants to meet me when he's next in New York. I agree to meet him at his restaurant in the Essex House, where everything in the place is so prim and proper. I introduce myself, but no one seems to know why I'm here. Finally I'm led into a big room with just three chairs. One of Ducasse's directors sits in one chair and I sit across from him. Then Ducasse walks in. He sits down and immediately starts speaking rapidly in French (I've never wanted a translator so badly in my life!), then his phone rings; someone on the other end of the line tells him he's just been awarded three Michelin stars. Suddenly both men are talking loudly, their phones ringing, the room is noisy and chaotic, and I'm just sitting there. In the middle of it all Ducasse seems to remember me; he turns and says simply, "You're coming to France. I'll see you in Paris." And he leaves the room. His director explains that Ducasse is impressed with my style of food, the attention to detail and the pristine kitchen at Yumcha. He says something about passion and professionalism. I tell him that I appreciate it immensely, it's a huge honor, but explain that I have a job, and don't see how this would work out.

He doesn't seem remotely troubled by this and we say our goodbyes. Now for the curve in the road: Two weeks later, Yumcha closed. Before I knew it, I was being whisked away to stage in Ducasse's Louis XV restaurant in Monte Carlo. I'd never seen a kitchen so beautiful. The chefs were a sea of white, all moving as if they were in a ballet, graceful and fluid. There was an amazing speed to everything they did, but also incredible precision, concentration, and passion—being there in the midst of this made all the doubts I had about past decisions vanish. Leaving Jean-Georges, going to Yumcha, every choice I'd questioned in my career was irrelevant now.

Everything that had happened was leading up to this magnificent moment—I was exactly where I was supposed to be. Sure, I'd known all my life that Alain Ducasse is one of the worlds' greatest chefs, I just had no idea how beautifully he'd spice up my life.

# Pineapple and Celery Salad
# with Sambal

**Serves: 4    Time: About 20 minutes    Flavors: Spicy/Sweet/Acidic**

This dish was created in the Nyonya style—a combination of Malaysian and Chinese influences. The key is the shrimp paste, also known as belacan, which adds an awesome umami flavor. This softens the sweetness and the acidity of the pineapple, while the texture and water content of the celery refreshes the palate.

1 tablespoon shrimp paste
4 cups chopped pineapple
1 cup chopped cucumber
2 stalks celery, cut into
  ¼-inch-thick slices
3 tablespoons chopped fresh
  cilantro

½ cup sambal
3 tablespoons olive oil
3 tablespoons lime juice
1 teaspoon kosher salt

**1** Put the shrimp paste in a small sauté pan and cook over medium heat until the fish aroma dissipates, about 3 minutes.

**2** Scrape the shrimp paste into a large bowl. Add the pineapple, cucumber, celery, cilantro, sambal, olive oil, lime juice, and salt and mix to combine. Place in the fridge to chill for about 20 minutes before serving.

Sambal is chile-based condiment used throughout Southeast Asia—you can find it in the ethnic food section of most grocery stores. It adds a beautiful spicy flavor to almost anything, but fair warning: It can be pretty hot, so if you're not used to cooking with it, be cautious at first.

# Spiced Watermelon Salad
## with Aleppo Pepper

**Serves: 4**   **Time: About 15 minutes**   **Flavors: Spicy/Sweet/Herbaceous**

I just love this dish. It reminds me of walking out into the garden back home in
Connecticut and picking a fresh watermelon for lunch—the vibrant green and
yellow striped skin, smooth and almost waxy on top with dirt still clinging to the
paler underside. With a perfect melon in hand, I'd head to our back porch and peel,
chop, and toss it with some fresh herbs. Then I'd hit it with some Aleppo pepper
and briny Greek olives for a vibrant, Mediterranean twist. Yum.

1 pound watermelon
1 teaspoon kosher salt
1 teaspoon fresh thyme
2 teaspoons ground Aleppo pepper
  (see Box, page 95)

1 tablespoon chopped salted Greek
  black olives
2 tablespoons olive oil
2 teaspoons chopped fresh mint

**1** Cut the watermelon into large cubes, remove and discard all the seeds, and place
in a large bowl. Add the salt, thyme, Aleppo pepper, olives, olive oil, and mint and
toss gently to combine. Drizzle with the olive oil, and garnish with the mint.

# Hot and Sour
# Chicken Fling

**Serves: 2 to 4    Time: About 45 minutes    Flavors: Spicy/Sweet/Sour**

This may be called a fling, but I guarantee it won't be a passing fancy. These super-crunchy wings are my idea of killer bar food. Warning: This page is going to get messy and sticky.

½ cup gochujang paste (see Box,
   page 70)
3 tablespoons Sriracha sauce
⅓ cup tamarind paste
⅓ cup red wine vinegar
2 tablespoons grated ginger

½ cup sugar
1½ cups all-purpose flour
2 cups water
grapeseed oil
1 pound chicken wings
fresh cilantro leaves

**1** Combine the gochujang paste, Sriracha sauce, tamarind paste, vinegar, ginger, and sugar in a small saucepan over medium-high heat. When the mixture comes to a boil, reduce the heat to a simmer and cook for 15 minutes, stirring occasionally. Transfer to a blender and purée until smooth. Place in a large bowl and set aside.

**2** In another large bowl, combine the flour and water and mix until smooth. Pour enough oil into a large pot to come about 3 inches up the sides. Turn the heat to high and bring to 325°F, as measured by a deep-fry or candy thermometer. Meanwhile, line a sheet pan with paper towels and put it by the stove to hold the chicken wings as they come out of the oil.

**3** When the oil is ready, dip each chicken wing in the batter. Working in batches so you don't overcrowd the pot, add the wings and fry for 8 to 10 minutes, until they are golden brown. Use a slotted spoon to remove the wings from the oil and transfer to the prepared sheet pan to drain any excess oil.

**4** Add the wings to the reserved bowl of sauce and toss gently to glaze. To serve, place the wings on a serving dish and garnish with the cilantro.

# Chicken Hot Dogs
# with Sweet and Sourkraut

Serves: 4   Time: About 1½ hours   Flavors: Spicy/Sour/Sweet

My grandfather Angelo used to take me to ballgames when I was a kid and I loved it—I was allowed to eat stuff that my parents would never allow at home! My son is a bit young still, but by the time he's old enough to go to games with me, I'm hoping they have sweet and sourkraut dogs just like this at the concession stands.

2 cups shredded cabbage
¼ cup kosher salt
3 cups seasoned rice wine vinegar
½ cup sugar
2 fresh bay leaves, torn
1 red Thai chile, minced

4 fresh thyme sprigs
10 juniper berries
4 chicken hot dogs
2 tablespoons grapeseed oil
4 brioche hot dog rolls

**1** Put the shredded cabbage in a large bowl with the salt and toss well; let sit for 30 minutes. Rinse the cabbage in cold water and drain off all excess water (a salad spinner works well here). Place the cabbage in a large bowl with the vinegar, sugar, bay leaves, chile, thyme, and juniper berries. Mix well and set aside.

**2** Meanwhile, bring a medium saucepan of water to a boil over medium-high heat and add the hot dogs. Cook the hot dogs for 10 minutes, drain, and pat dry with paper towels.

**3** Put a medium sauté pan over medium-high heat, add the oil to the pan, and sear the hot dogs until nicely browned on all sides, about 4 minutes total.

**4** Toast or warm the brioche rolls, place a hot dog in each, and top with the sourkraut to serve.

# Franco-Vietnamese Lobster Rolls with Crispy Shallots

Serves: 4   Time:  About 20 minutes   Flavors: Spicy/Sweet/Sour

Imagine the flavors of Southeast Asia and Maine all in one sandwich—this is my take on the classic New England lobster roll. The combination of luxurious lobster and crispy shallots is a textural adventure, and the slightly spicy mayo gives it just the right kick of heat. What more can I say?

½ cup mayonnaise
3 tablespoons seasoned rice
  wine vinegar
2 tablespoons sugar
3 tablespoons Sriracha sauce
¼ cup chopped red onions
3 tablespoons chopped fresh dill
1 tablespoon chopped fresh tarragon
½ teaspoon kosher salt

2 cups Maine lobster cut into
  large chunks
4 brioche rolls, cut in half
butter (optional)

Crispy Shallots
grapeseed oil
½ cup all-purpose flour
½ cup thinly sliced shallots
kosher salt

**1** In a medium bowl, combine the mayonnaise, vinegar, sugar, and Sriracha sauce and stir well until the sugar is completely dissolved. Add the onions, dill, tarragon, and salt and mix well. Add the lobster and toss to combine.

**2** Next, make the shallots: Pour enough oil into a small saucepan to come 1½ to 2 inches up the sides. Turn the heat to high and bring it to 325°F, as measured by a deep-fry or candy thermometer. While the oil heats, put the flour in a dish and dredge the shallots, shaking off any excess flour. Add the shallots to the oil and cook until golden, 2 to 3 minutes. Using a slotted spoon, transfer to paper towels to drain and sprinkle with salt.

**3** Toast the rolls and, for a bit more lusciousness, butter them. Top the bottom half of each roll with ½ cup or so of the lobster mixture and a nice sprinkling of shallots, replace the top half of the roll, and serve.

# Blackened Swordfish
## with Spiced Pepper Relish

Serves: 4    Time: About 1½ hours    Flavors: Spicy/Briny/Sweet

When I was a kid we spent summers on Cape Cod and I used to eat a lot of swordfish. It was usually a very simple preparation—just grilled fish with salt and pepper. Then later I spent time in Provence and was captivated by the floral notes of the fresh thyme that grows everywhere, the amazing olive oils, and the luscious red peppers in the markets. I wanted to bring all these spectacular flavors together somehow, but I didn't want a pure French tapanade—I wanted to balance the brininess of the olives with some sweetness. And here you have it.

4 red peppers
3 tablespoons extra virgin olive oil,
  plus more as needed
3 tablespoons diced green
  Cerignola olives
1 red Thai chile, minced
1 teaspoon fresh thyme leaves

¼ teaspoon kosher salt, plus more
  as needed
1 teaspoon sugar
zest of 1 lemon
grapeseed oil for brushing
4 swordfish steaks (about 1½ pounds
  total)
freshly ground black pepper

1 Using tongs, carefully hold a pepper over a burner turned to high heat and gradually turn the pepper to blacken each side thoroughly. When the pepper is well charred, place it in a large bowl and repeat with the remaining peppers. Cover the bowl with plastic wrap and let stand until the skins are loosened, about 30 minutes. When the peppers are cool enough to handle, peel off the skins, remove the stems, seeds, and core and finely chop the peppers. Place in a large bowl with 3 tablespoons of olive oil, the olives, chile, thyme, ¼ teaspoon salt, sugar, and lemon zest and stir to combine. Set aside.

2 Heat a grill to high and brush the grates with oil, or heat a grill pan over medium-high heat and brush with oil. Season the swordfish with salt and pepper. Cook the swordfish for about 2 minutes on the first side; flip and repeat with other side. The fish is done when it's opaque all the way through and can be easily pierced with a paring knife.

3 To serve, place each steak on a plate and top with a generous dollop of the relish.

# Spiced Shrimp Po' Boy

**Serves: 4   Time: About 1 hour   Flavors: Spicy/Salty/Smoky**

When it comes to flavor, I'm all about fresh herbs and exotic spices, but sometimes what you really want is right there in your pantry just waiting to be jazzed up and used in a totally new way. Take Old Bay seasoning. Sure it's a classic American crab boil blend, but add some sultry Asian flavors and you've got an amazing combo that's part southern, part Southeast Asian, and totally yummy.

Old Bay Salt
¼ cup Old Bay seasoning spice
2 tablespoons paprika
2 tablespoons kosher salt

Thai Chile Relish
2 tablespoons grapeseed oil
1 cup diced onion
3 tablespoons sugar
½ teaspoon kosher salt
1 cup diced green pepper
2 tablespoons minced jalapeño chile
1 teaspoon minced green Thai chile
½ cup seasoned rice wine vinegar

2 cups medium shrimp (21/25)
3 tablespoons cornstarch
½ cup all-purpose flour
½ teaspoon kosher salt
½ cup water
grapeseed oil
1 cup shredded iceberg lettuce
¼ cup fresh mint leaves
¼ cup fresh cilantro leaves
4 potato hot dog buns

**1** First make the Old Bay salt: Combine the Old Bay, paprika, and salt in a small bowl and set aside.

**2** Then make the Thai Chile Relish: Put the oil in a medium sauté pan over low heat and sweat the onions until soft and transparent, 4 to 5 minutes. Add the sugar and salt and stir to combine. Add the green pepper, jalapeño, and Thai chile and cook for another 2 minutes. Add the vinegar, turn the heat to high, and reduce the liquid until it glazes the vegetables, another 3 minutes. Remove from the heat and chill in the refrigerator for at least 10 minutes.

**3** Pat the shrimp dry with paper towels to remove any excess water. Put the cornstarch in a shallow dish or bowl; dredge the shrimp in the cornstarch until lightly but thoroughly coated.

**4** In a medium bowl, combine the flour and salt with the water and mix well. Pour enough oil into a large pot to just coat the bottom of the pot. Line a sheet pan with paper towels and put it by the stove to hold the shrimp as they come out of the oil.

**5** When the oil is hot, dip the shrimp in the batter and, working in batches, add them to the pan. Fry the shrimp until golden brown, about 2 minutes. Using a slotted spoon, carefully remove the shrimp from the oil and drain them on the prepared sheet pan. Immediately sprinkle the shrimp generously with the reserved Old Bay salt.

**6** In a large bowl, toss the lettuce, mint, and cilantro together. Lightly toast the hot dog buns; mound a generous handful of the salad on the bottom of each bun, top with some of the fried shrimp, and garnish with a dollop of the relish.

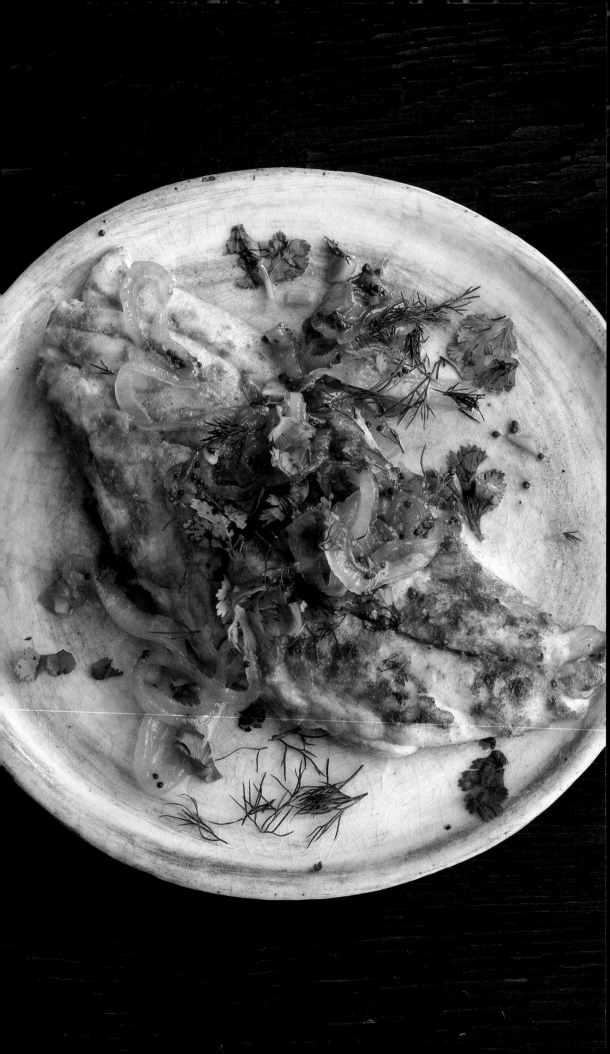

# Red Snapper
## a la Chaca

Serves: 4    Time: About 1½ hours    Flavors: Spicy/Sweet/Herbaceous

The flavors in this dish are spectacular: the briny fish sauce, the sweet yet acidic onions, and the herbaceous dill and cilantro are a surprising but totally satisfying combo. If you're like me and love a bit of heat, add a touch of Sriracha sauce at the end with the garnish—the spiciness is awesome with the saltiness of the fish.

3 tablespoons ground turmeric
2 tablespoons fish sauce
four 6-ounce red snapper fillets
2 tablespoons grapeseed oil
2 tablespoons chopped fresh dill
2 tablespoons chopped fresh cilantro

Pickled Onions
2 tablespoons grapeseed oil

3 cups sliced onions
3 tablespoons chopped garlic
1 tablespoon mustard seeds
1 tablespoon ground turmeric
½ cup plus 2 tablespoons sugar
2 tablespoons kosher salt
1 cup red wine vinegar

**1** In a dish large enough to hold the fish in a single layer, combine the turmeric and fish sauce. Add the fish, gently coating it in the marinade. Cover and refrigerate for at least 1 hour and up to 8 hours.

**2** Meanwhile, make the Pickled Onions: In a large sauté pan, heat the oil over medium heat. Add the onions and garlic and sweat until soft and aromatic, 5 to 8 minutes, lowering the heat if necessary to keep them from coloring. Add the mustard seeds and turmeric and toast until just aromatic, about 2 minutes. Add the sugar and salt and combine well, then add the vinegar and deglaze the bottom of the pan. Continue to cook until the liquid reduces and the onions are lightly glazed, 8 to 10 minutes. Remove from the heat and let come to room temperature.

**3** When you're ready to cook, heat the oil over medium-high heat in a sauté pan large enough to hold the fish in a single layer. When hot, cook the fish until the first side is golden and slightly crisp, 3 to 4 minutes, depending on the thickness of the fillets. Turn the fish over and repeat with the other side. When the fish is cooked through, serve it topped with a mound of the Pickled Onions and garnished with the dill and cilantro.

# Wok-Charred Baby Bok Choy
## with Finger Chiles

Serves: 4    Time: About 15 minutes    Flavors: Spicy/Umami/Astringent

Your initial instinct in this recipe will be to turn down the heat after adding the ginger and garlic—ignore that instinct! Instead, be quick on your feet and increase the heat, then add the bok choy and the remaining ingredients. This is all about speed. The bok choy should be slightly wilted yet crispy and crunchy at the same time. This is how an authentic Cantonese-style stir-fry goes down, and once you get used to the technique you'll be all set.

3 tablespoons grapeseed oil
1 teaspoon chopped ginger
1 teaspoon chopped garlic
1 pound baby bok choy, halved
   lengthwise

1 teaspoon oyster sauce
2 tablespoons water
1 finger chile, finely chopped
1 teaspoon toasted sesame oil

**1** Place a wok over medium heat and add the oil. When the oil is hot, add the ginger and garlic and cook until lightly golden, stirring frequently, 1 to 2 minutes. Increase the heat to high, add the bok choy, oyster sauce, and water and continue tossing as the mixture cooks. When the bok choy begins to wilt and has turned bright green, add the chile, toss again, and remove from the heat. Finish with the sesame oil and serve immediately.

# Piri Piri
# Chile Relish

**Makes: About 2 cups    Time: About 30 minutes    Flavors: Spicy/Sweet/Acidic**

Piri piri means "pepper pepper," or "red devil" in Portuguese. Typically you find piri piri sauces in Mozambique, which was settled by the Portuguese. It's a very traditional condiment that I've turned into a spicy relish—one that you can use on almost anything: chicken, fish, burgers, even just a spread on a toasted baguette for a spicy bruschetta.

¼ cup Sriracha sauce
¼ cup gochujang paste (see Box, page 70)
1 cup seasoned rice wine vinegar
½ cup sugar
1 teaspoon kosher salt

3 tablespoons grapeseed oil
2 cups finely chopped onions
1 cup finely chopped red pepper
1 cup finely chopped green pepper
4 red Thai chiles, minced
1 jalapeño pepper, minced

**1** In a medium bowl, combine the Sriracha sauce, gochujang paste, vinegar, sugar, and salt. Whisk until the sugar dissolves and set aside.

**2** Place the oil in a large sauté pan set over medium-high heat. When hot, add the onions, reduce the heat to medium, and cook until they begin to soften but don't color, about 5 minutes. Add the peppers and cook for another 2 minutes. Add the Thai chiles, jalapeño, and the reserved liquid and increase the heat to high.

**3** Stirring frequently, allow the liquid to reduce and glaze the vegetables, about 4 minutes, then remove from the heat, and let cool. Serve as desired or transfer to an airtight container and keep refrigerated for up to 2 weeks.

# Curried
## Pots de Creme

Serves: 6    Time: About 1 hour    Flavors: Spicy/Sweet/Astringent

This is my way of bringing an Indian flair to a French classic—it's the ultimate fusion of spicy and creamy. Simply put, it's luscious.

5 cardamom pods
1 cinnamon stick
¼ teaspoon cumin seeds
¼ teaspoon ground turmeric
1¼ cups whole milk

1 cup heavy cream
6 egg yolks
5 tablespoons sugar
fresh cilantro leaves

1 Preheat the oven to 350°F.

2 In a small skillet over low heat, lightly toast each of the spices, one at a time starting with the largest and adding them to the pan in order of decreasing size; be sure to end with the ground turmeric. Cool the spices thoroughly before grinding them to a fine powder in a spice grinder. Set aside.

3 In a medium saucepan, bring the milk and cream to a boil over medium-high heat.

4 In a large bowl, whisk the yolks until well combined. Add the sugar and the reserved curry powder. Add the milk and cream to the egg mixture a bit at a time (this is called tempering)—you don't want the hot milk to cook the eggs. Combine well.

5 Transfer the custard to six 4-ounce ramekins. Place the ramekins in a roasting pan and carefully add enough hot water to the pan to come halfway up the sides of the ramekins. Bake for 30 to 45 minutes, until just set. Remove the ramekins from the water and let cool on a rack. Garnish with the cilantro, and serve.

# Spiced Ketchup

Makes: About 2½ cups   Time: About 45 minutes   Flavors: Spicy/Smoky/Sweet

This ketchup is an incredibly tantalizing condiment. It's grounded in sweetness but offers up an entire gamut of different spice notes—it's absolutely perfect on a beautiful piece of grilled meat, as the spices cut through the fat and enliven your taste buds.

3 tablespoons grapeseed oil
¼ cup chopped shallots
1 tablespoon grated ginger
1 tablespoon grated Asian or Bosc pear
3 tablespoons chipotle chiles
  in adobo sauce

6 allspice berries
6 cloves
1 tablespoon ground Aleppo pepper
1 tablespoon ground Ancho chile
2 cups prepared ketchup
¼ cup sugar

**1** In a medium saucepan, heat the oil over low heat. Add the shallots and sweat until they are soft and transparent, 3 to 5 minutes. Add the ginger, pear, chipotles, allspice berries, cloves, Aleppo pepper, and ancho chile and cook for 5 minutes, or until the mixture is very aromatic.

**2** Add the ketchup and sugar to the pan, increase the heat to medium-high, and bring the mixture to a boil. Reduce the heat to low and simmer for 15 minutes. Transfer the mixture to a blender and purée until smooth. Let cool and use as desired, or store in an airtight container in the fridge for up to 3 months.

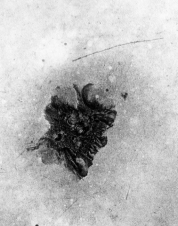

# Jalapeño and Lemongrass
## Vinaigrette

**Makes:** 1½ cups    **Time:** 20 minutes    **Flavors:** Spicy/Herbaceous/Sweet

This recipe is perfect for marinating tofu before you grill it. It's also beautiful on greens, grilled corn, fish, even lobster. I also love to drizzle it over fresh watermelon for a quick snack.

½ cup sugar
1½ cups water
1 stalk lemongrass, smashed and chopped
1 jalapeño chile, chopped

1 teaspoon ground turmeric
1 tablespoon finely chopped cilantro stems
2 tablespoons olive oil

Combine the sugar, water, and lemongrass in a small saucepan over medium-high heat. When it comes to a boil, reduce to a simmer. Add the jalapeño, turmeric, and cilantro and cook for 2 minutes. Transfer to a blender and purée until smooth. Strain the mixture through a fine sieve, add the olive oil, and chill for at least 20 minutes or until cold. Use as desired or transfer to an airtight container and store in the fridge for up to 3 days.

Puffed Pita Chips with Toasted Nigella

# Garden Salad with Soy-Truffle Vinaigrette

Buttered Potato Noodles with Soy Glaze

# Chocolate-Braised Short Ribs

Seared Sirloin Steak with Garlic-Soy Infusion

# Fiery Korean Satays

Cocoa-Rubbed Beef Tacos

Tuna Kebabs with Cherry Tomatoes and Feta

# Grilled Watermelon with Chinese A-1 Sauce

## Chocolate Parsnip Purée

Turmeric Cauliflower Pickles

## "Earth Rub" Spice Mix

# Earthy 8

# Earthy | Planting the Seeds

**I don't remember the moment I realized I wanted to be a chef,** but I remember when I first said it out loud to someone I respected.

I was in my first year at the CIA—the Culinary Institute of America—when I walked into President Ferdinand Metz's office, and asked his secretary if I could speak with him. She smiled and asked why. I said that I simply needed to talk to him, that it was very important. No, she couldn't give me an appointment, but she could arrange for me to go with another class to a meeting he would be attending. When I got to the meeting I walked right up to him and said, "I'm Angelo Sosa. Remember this name because I'm going to be the youngest master chef in the world." And that was it. I turned and walked away! It was totally ridiculous, but that's how I felt. I needed Ferdinand Metz to know who I was: a very young, very passionate, and in retrospect, pretty naïve kid.

It's a funny story now—but I'm not embarrassed by it. At that moment in time I followed my heart and did what I felt I had to do: I needed the powers that be to understand that I was in it to win it. It's just how I was raised. Some kids have pictures of girls in their lockers; I had pictures of Gray Kunz and Jean-Georges. To me these were men worthy of worship, they were the greatest living chefs and I yearned to be like them one day.

I began my first culinary program at a local community college. I would get up every morning at four-thirty to be at work at the corporate kitchen at Cigna Healthcare by six, sometimes catch a nap in the parking lot if I got in early, and then leave work and go to school until nine at night. I was operating on about four hours of sleep each day, but it was okay—I was in culinary school. And I was lucky: I had a mentor who helped push me along. Chef Mark, my chef at Cigna, encouraged me to enter various culinary competitions, and he helped me get into the CIA.

When I first started at the CIA I was like a rookie cop who wanted his gun. I was so antsy to wear chef's whites I could barely stand it. I would go to the Escoffier Room, the renowned French restaurant on campus, and hound the head chef, Chef Chenus, to work in his kitchen. He was a feared chef, standing like a statue with his toque slightly tilted on his head at the front of the kitchen, and I was like a bulldog that wouldn't get lost. I kept showing up every day after my classes, until finally he allowed me to watch the other students, gradually getting to do little tasks and integrating myself into his kitchen. I was probably a real pain in the ass, but he could see I was dedicated.

Dedicated for sure, but it was more than that—I had gone from being passionate about cooking to being obsessed by it. After going to class all morning and working for Chef Chenus all afternoon, I'd go to practice for the Junior Culinary Team until one in the morning. After that, instead of going home to sleep, I'd be so amped up and invigorated that I'd go sit by the train tracks along the Hudson River. I'd just stare up at the stars wondering: Would I be good

enough, could I be the best, what more could I be doing? I needed to become a chef—a great chef. My whole being was about making this dream come true.

And it did come true. Thanks to Chef Mark, Chef Ligouri, Chef Chenus, Jean-Georges, Christan Betrand, and Alain Ducasse. I've been very lucky to have all of these great men as teachers and mentors. I'm not sure what they saw in me—a kid from a small town in Connecticut—but I'm so thankful they saw something that I hadn't always seen in myself. It's given me roots, the grounding I've needed to keep striving, to keep trying to be the best chef (and person) I can be.

# Puffed Pita Chips
# with Toasted Nigella

Serves: 8   Time: About 1 hour   Flavors: Earthy/Nutty/Salty

Nigella, from the Middle East, is also known as black onion seed. It has a beautiful aroma: fragrant and musty, similar to basmati rice. When paired with something warm, the fragrance lingers, like freshly made pastries first thing in the morning. These chips are awesome as a snack on their own or tossed in a tomato salad for a Middle Eastern twist on panzanella.

1 tablespoon active dry yeast
2 tablespoons sugar
⅓ cup warm water
1 cup all-purpose flour, plus more
   as needed

2½ teaspoons kosher salt
olive oil
2 teaspoons nigella seeds, toasted

**1** In a medium bowl, combine the yeast, sugar, and water and let stand for about 10 minutes, until the yeast becomes foamy. Add the flour and ½ teaspoon of the salt and mix well. Use your hands to gather the dough and knead it gently on a lightly floured surface until it comes together into a smooth ball. If the dough seems too dry, add a bit of water a tablespoon at a time; if it seems too wet, add a sprinkling of flour.

**2** Oil the inside of a medium bowl, transfer the dough to the bowl, cover tightly with plastic wrap, and let rest in a warm area for 15 minutes.

**3** Lightly dust your work surface with flour. Use a rolling pin to roll the dough out into an ⅛-inch-thick rectangle. Use a pizza cutter or sharp knife to cut the dough into ½ x ½-inch squares.

**4** Pour enough oil into a large pot to come about 3 inches up the sides. Turn the heat to high and bring to 325°F, as measured by a deep-fry or candy thermometer. Meanwhile, line a sheet pan with paper towels and put it by the stove to hold the pita chips as they come out of the oil.

**5** When the oil is ready, drop the squares of dough into the pot, and lightly dunk them with a slotted spoon to keep them submerged until they just turn golden and puff up, |about 2 minutes. Carefully transfer to the prepared sheet pan to drain any excess oil. While they're still hot, sprinkle with the remaining 2 teaspoons of salt and the toasted nigella seeds.

# Garden Salad with
## Soy-Truffle Vinaigrette

**Serves: 4** **Time: 15 minutes** **Flavors: Earthy/Umami/Herbaceous**

I know it sounds simple, but this salad rocks. The dill is the glue—it ties all the flavors together. You just have to try it.

1 small head green lola rosa lettuce
1 small head red lola rosa lettuce
1 small head baby romaine lettuce
2 cups arugula

1 cup light soy sauce
¼ cup lemon juice
1 tablespoon olive oil
2 tablespoons truffle oil
3 tablespoons chopped fresh dill
freshly ground black pepper

**1** Separate the leaves of the lettuce and place all the greens in a large bowl.

**2** In a small bowl, combine the soy sauce, lemon juice, olive oil, and truffle oil and whisk well. Dress the salad with the vinaigrette, sprinkle with the dill, season with pepper, and serve.

# Buttered Potato Noodles
# with Soy Glaze

**Serves: 6    Time: About 20 minutes    Flavors: Earthy/Salty/Astringent**

The whole idea here is to up the ante on the potatoes by making them resemble spaghetti or pappardelle: lovely long, thin potato noodles. How thick your noodles are depends on the blade you choose to use for your mandoline. It's a super-cool way to add finesse to a staple ingredient.

¼ cup light soy sauce
2 tablespoons water
1 tablespoon minced garlic
8 Yukon gold potatoes, peeled

3 tablespoons unsalted butter
freshly ground black pepper
2 tablespoons chopped fresh chives

**1** Combine the soy sauce, water, and garlic in a blender and purée until smooth. Strain and transfer to a large saucepan and set aside.

**2** Use a mandoline to shred the potatoes lengthwise so they resemble long noodles. Add the potatoes to the pan along with the butter and place over medium heat. Cook for about 2 minutes, or until the potatoes are glazed in the liquid. Remove from the heat, transfer to a serving dish, season with pepper, and garnish with the chives.

A mandoline is one of those kitchen tools that you may not use every day, but when you need it, you really need it. It's the best way to get those lovely, almost see-through slices of potato or those paper-thin pieces of fennel. And you can use different blades for different shapes. Just be careful—the blades are very sharp and it's easy to cut yourself.

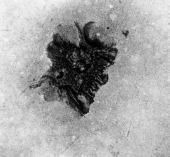

# Chocolate Braised
## Short Ribs

**Serves: 4   Time: About 3½ hours   Flavors: Earthy/Sweet/Bitter**

This dish is inspired by Mexican mole—a savory chocolate sauce that originated in Oaxaca. I love cooking savory ingredients with chocolate because the contrast is so unexpected. In this dish, the sweet yet bitter flavor of chocolate brings out a luscious richness in the meaty ribs, and the spice blend has a smoky aroma that just adds to the seductiveness. Serve with a bold, acidic salad, like sliced radishes dressed with a spicy citrus vinaigrette.

Spice Blend
**one 2-inch piece cinnamon**
**4 dried chipotle chiles**
**½ teaspoon whole cloves**
**1 teaspoon allspice berries**
**¼ cup unsweetened cocoa powder**
**3 tablespoons kosher salt**

**5 pounds boneless beef short ribs**
**⅓ cup grapeseed oil**

**2 cups ketchup**
**1½ cups sugar**
**1 cup red wine vinegar**
**½ cup tamarind paste**
**1 cup unsweetened cocoa powder**
**1 gallon water**
**fresh mint or cilantro leaves**

**1** First make the Spice Blend: In a dry sauté pan over medium heat, lightly toast the cinnamon, chipotles, cloves, and allspice, starting with the largest spice first and gradually adding in order of decreasing size. Continue cooking, shaking the pan occasionally, until they're aromatic, 3 to 4 minutes total. Cool completely, then grind the spices in a spice grinder until very fine. In a small bowl, combine the spices with the cocoa powder and salt and set aside.

**2** Pat the ribs dry with paper towels. Rub with the prepared spice blend and brush lightly with the oil. Place in a dish and marinate for at least 1 hour at room temperature or up to 8 hours in the fridge.

**3** Add the remaining oil to a large, deep pot set over high heat. When the oil shimmers, sear the ribs on all sides until well browned, 15 to 20 minutes. Work in batches if necessary to make sure the ribs brown and don't steam.

**4** Preheat the oven to 300°F. Meanwhile, in a large saucepan, combine the ketchup, sugar, vinegar, tamarind paste, cocoa powder, and water. Bring the mixture to a simmer over medium-high heat, stirring occasionally, until the sugar dissolves. When all the ribs have been browned, return them all to the large pot, pour the ketchup mixture over the ribs, cover with foil or a lid, and braise in the oven for 2½ hours, or until fork tender.

**5** When the ribs are done, remove them from the liquid and put them on a sheet pan. Carefully strain the braising liquid through a fine-mesh sieve into a medium saucepan. Put over medium-high heat and reduce, stirring frequently, until it's the consistency of heavy cream and coats the back of spoon. Remove from the heat.

**6** Turn the oven to broil and brush the reserved ribs with the thickened sauce. Put them in the broiler for 2 to 3 minutes to lacquer the exterior, keeping an eye on them to make sure they don't burn. Garnish with fresh mint or cilantro and serve.

# Seared Sirloin Steak
## with Garlic-Soy Infusion

Serves: 4   Time: About 30 minutes   Flavors: Earthy/Astringent/Umami

Don't let the simplicity of this steak put you off—the depth of the char flavor combined with the butter offers a ton of voluptuousness to the meat, and the umami flavor of the soy melded with the sweet garlic is gorgeous. My advice? Whip up a batch of my Turmeric Cauliflower Pickles (page 184) to serve with this—the acidity will cut through the richness of the steak beautifully.

¼ cup light soy sauce
3 tablespoons Worcestershire sauce
1 tablespoon thinly sliced garlic
½ cup (1 stick) unsalted butter
four 8-ounce sirloin steaks

kosher salt
freshly ground black pepper
3 tablespoons grapeseed oil
1 tablespoon fresh thyme leaves

1 In a saucepan, combine the soy sauce, Worcestershire sauce, garlic, and half the butter over medium heat. Cook for 5 to 7 minutes, until the mixture thickens and coats the back of a spoon. Remove from the heat and set aside.

2 Meanwhile, pat the steaks dry with paper towels and season with salt and pepper. Heat a large sauté pan over medium-high heat and add the oil. When the oil is hot, add the steaks to the pan and cook until nicely colored, 2 to 4 minutes depending on how thick the steaks are. Turn the steaks and add the remaining butter to the pan along with the thyme. Use a spoon to baste the steaks with the butter-thyme mixture as they cook.

3 When the steaks are done, remove from the heat, spoon any remaining thyme and pan juices over them, and let sit for 2 minutes. To serve, slice against the grain and drizzle with the garlic-soy sauce.

# Fiery Korean
## Satays

**Serves: 6 to 8   Time: 1 hour   Flavors: Earthy/Spicy/Smoky**

My newest love is Korean cuisine. From Flushing Queens to K-town in mid-Manhattan, I'm always searching out new restaurants to try. But when it comes to bulgogi—which is basically what this recipe is—I love making it myself. There's nothing like turning the backyard into a Korean BBQ. And, as far as I'm concerned, grilling isn't just for warm weather. In the winter, the combination of the hot fire, the cold air, and the smoky aroma of these satays is truly a full sensory experience.

½ cup gochujang paste
  (see Box, page 70)
¼ cup Sriracha sauce
3 tablespoons sesame oil
¼ cup light soy sauce

3 tablespoons grapeseed oil,
  plus more for the grill
¼ cup seasoned rice wine vinegar
¼ cup sugar
one 2-pound pork butt

**1** Combine the gochujang paste, Sriracha sauce, sesame oil, soy sauce, grapeseed oil, vinegar, and sugar in a large, wide dish and stir until the sugar dissolves and the mixture is smooth.

**2** Using a very sharp knife, slice the meat into ⅛-inch-thick slices, about 3 to 4 inches in length. Add the meat to the dish with the marinade and let stand for about 30 minutes at room temperature.

**3** Meanwhile, soak wooden skewers in water for at least 10 minutes (this helps prevent splintering). When the meat has marinated, carefully thread the slices onto the soaked wooden skewers and reserve the marinade for brushing the meat while it grills.

**4** Heat a grill to high, or a grill pan over medium-high heat. Oil the grill or grill pan and place the skewers over the hottest part. Cook the satays, turning as needed every minute or so, and brushing with the reserved marinade with each turn, 2 to 3 minutes total. Serve immediately.

# Cocoa-Rubbed
## Beef Tacos

Serves: 4    Time: About 1½ hours    Flavors: Earthy/Bitter/Sweet

Cocoa and beef are a great combination. The chocolate undertones combined with the richness of the red meat are glorious wrapped up with the charred sweetness of the corn tortilla. The pickled vegetables and the cilantro add a welcome acidity and brightness—it all just works magically together.

1 tablespoon cumin seeds
1 tablespoon coriander seeds
¼ cup unsweetened cocoa powder
¼ cup kosher salt
½ pound skirt steak
3 tablespoons grapeseed oil
1 cup shredded carrots
1 cup shredded cucumber

1 cup bean sprouts
1 cup gochujang paste (see Box, page 70)
3 tablespoons sesame oil
¼ cup seasoned rice wine vinegar
3 tablespoons sugar
8 good-quality corn tortillas
fresh cilantro sprigs

**1** In a small dry sauté pan over medium heat, lightly toast the coriander and cumin seeds until aromatic, about 2 minutes. Let cool completely, then grind the spices, cocoa powder, and 1 tablespoon of the salt in a spice grinder until very fine.

**2** Pat the beef dry with paper towels and rub the meat with the oil and the spice mixture until thoroughly coated. (Reserve any extra spice rub in an airtight container to use later.) Let stand at room temperature for 30 minutes to marinate.

**3** Combine the carrots, cucumber, bean sprouts, and the remaining 3 tablespoons of salt in a large bowl and let stand for 30 minutes. Rinse the vegetables, squeeze out any excess liquid, and set aside. Meanwhile, combine the gochujang paste, sesame oil, vinegar, and sugar in a large bowl. Add the vegetables to the bowl and toss well to combine.

**4** Heat a grill to medium-high or a grill pan over medium-high heat and cook the meat until well charred on the outside but still pink on the inside, about 2 minutes per side. Let rest for a couple of minutes before thinly slicing against the grain.

**5** Wrap the tortillas in a damp kitchen towel and steam them in the microwave until soft, about 1 minute or less. Using tongs, carefully flash each tortilla over a burner, turning once, to release the corn flavor.

**6** To serve, place a spoonful of the marinated vegetables on each tortilla, add a few slices of the beef, and garnish with a sprig of cilantro.

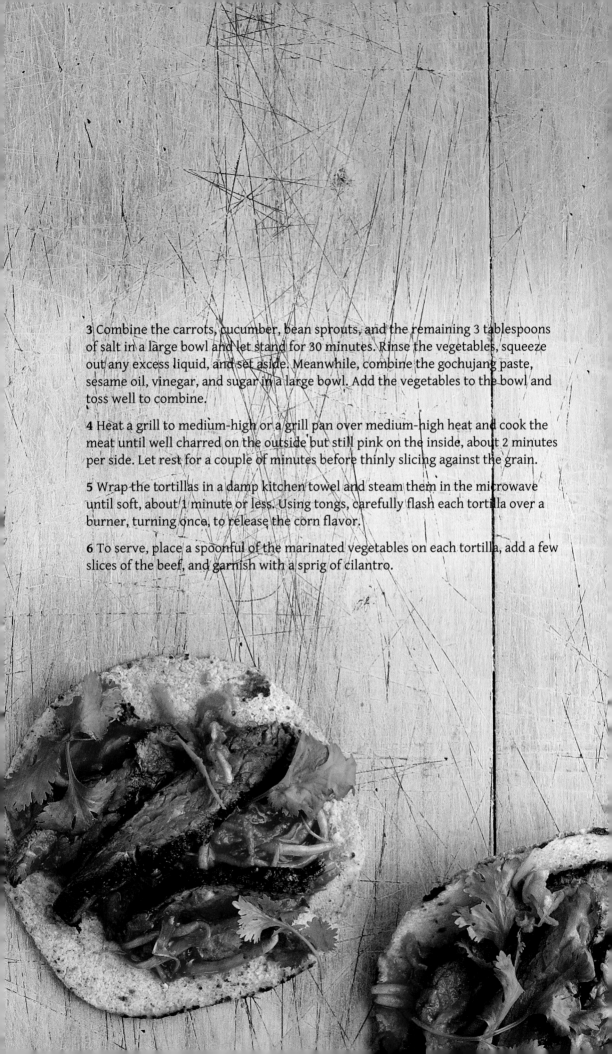

# Tuna Kebabs
## with Cherry Tomatoes and Feta

Serves: 4    Time: About 30 minutes    Flavors: Earthy/Herbaceous/Astringent

Typically people think of kebabs as a cooked dish, but this is a great raw summer treat. It's really all about the purity of the ingredients: beautiful tuna, sweet summer watermelon, and fresh herbs. And believe this: Contrary to what people believe, cheese and fish are lovely together.

½ pound sashimi-grade tuna
½ pound wedge of seedless watermelon
fresh oregano leaves
6 cherry tomatoes, halved
fresh Thai basil leaves

1 cup feta cheese
3 tablespoons olive oil
3 tablespoons lemon juice
fleur de sel or other high-quality salt
freshly ground black pepper

1 Soak 12 wooden skewers in water for at least 10 minutes to help prevent splintering.

2 Meanwhile, cut the tuna and watermelon into ½ x ½-inch cubes. Thread a piece of tuna on each skewer, followed by an oregano leaf, a tomato half, a Thai basil leaf, and a cube of watermelon. Repeat with all the skewers and refrigerate until ready to serve.

3 Combine the feta, olive oil, and lemon juice in a blender and purée until smooth.

4 To serve, sprinkle the skewers with a bit of fleur de sel and a grind of pepper and drizzle with the feta dressing.

# Grilled Watermelon
## with Chinese A-1 Sauce

Serves: 4   Time: About 20 minutes   Flavors: Earthy/Sweet/Spicy

Yes, it works. And while it may not be your first instinct to grill watermelon, trust me, the contrast of the sweetness of the fruit and the deep char of the grill is amazing. The melon takes on the composition of a steak while the salty and savory flavor of the A-1 sauce adds a familiar but unexpected twist.

1 cup A-1 steak sauce
3 tablespoons light soy sauce
2 tablespoons gochujang paste
  (see Box, page 70)
1 tablespoon toasted sesame oil
grapeseed oil

½ pound seedless watermelon,
  cut into ½-inch-thick steaks
¼ teaspoon fleur de sel or other
  high-quality salt
fresh cilantro leaves
3 tablespoons olive oil

1 Combine the A-1 sauce, soy sauce, gochujang paste, and sesame oil in a small saucepan over medium heat. Bring to a boil, stir to combine, and remove from the heat. Transfer to a blender, purée until smooth, and set aside.

2 Lightly oil a grill or grill pan and heat it to medium-high. Place the melon on the hottest part of the grill. Cook until grill marks appear, 1 to 2 minutes each side. Transfer to a serving dish, sprinkle with the fleur de sel, drizzle the A-1 sauce around the melon, garnish with the cilantro, and finish with the olive oil.

# Chocolate
# Parsnip Purée

**Serves: 6    Time: About 30 minutes    Flavors: Earthy/Sweet/Bitter**

Cocoa puffs—yes you heard right, the cereal—inspired me to create this dish. When you eat the puffs the sweetness of the cocoa infuses the milk, and that combo of flavors is literally the same in this recipe. Want to live lavish? Garnish this with a handful of actual cocoa puffs!

4 cups peeled and chopped parsnips

2 cups water

1 cup whole milk

¼ cup sugar

1 teaspoon kosher salt

¼ cup unsweetened cocoa powder

2 tablespoons unsalted butter

**1** Combine the parsnips, water, milk, half of the sugar, and the salt in a medium saucepan over medium-high heat. Bring to a boil, then reduce to a simmer and cook until the parsnips are tender, about 10 minutes.

**2** Drain the parsnips, reserving about ½ cup of the cooking liquid, and transfer to a blender. Add the cocoa powder, the remaining half of the sugar, and the butter to the blender and purée until smooth; if necessary, add a bit of the reserved liquid to loosen the mixture. Reheat if necessary and serve as a side dish.

# Turmeric
## Cauliflower Pickles

Serves: 12   Time: 1 day   Flavors: Earthy/Acidic/Herbaceous

This is the essence of India in a jar. Turmeric is a used as a dye for silks in India, but it's also a traditional ingredient in Indian dishes. It has a deep astringent flavor, with a hint of mustiness. I find it adds a ton of depth to food, especially in curries. Here I use it to add both flavor and a gorgeous amber color to these pickles, which I like to serve with any type of grilled meat, fish, and especially burgers.

8 cardamom pods
4 allspice berries
1 tablespoon mustard seeds
2 tablespoons ground turmeric
3 cups seasoned rice wine vinegar

1 cup sugar
2 teaspoons kosher salt
6 fresh dill sprigs
2 red Thai chiles, halved
2 heads cauliflower, cut into small florets

**1** In a medium dry sauté pan over medium heat, lightly toast the cardamom pods, allspice berries, mustard seeds, and turmeric, starting with the largest spice first and gradually adding the others in order of decreasing size. Continue cooking, shaking the pan occasionally, until they're all aromatic, 3 to 4 minutes total. Let cool.

**2** In a large bowl, combine the vinegar, sugar, salt, dill, chiles, and toasted spices. Add the cauliflower to the pickling liquid and stir to combine. Spoon the cauliflower and marinade into airtight containers and let stand for at least 24 hours before using. These will hold up to 1 month in the fridge.

# "Earth Rub"
## Spice Mix

**Makes: About ¾ cup**   **Time: About 15 minutes**   **Flavors: Earthy/Smoky/Nutty**

When you first taste this spice blend you get the subtle menthol flavor of the black cardamom, then the smoke prevails. The sweetness of the Aleppo pepper is totally luscious, and the oils of the coriander and nigella round it all out. Worth noting: I would only use this recipe with red meat—it can stand up next to the intense flavors.

2 black cardamom pods  
2 tablespoons black peppercorns  
¼ cup coriander seeds

2 tablespoons nigella seeds  
2 tablespoons ground Aleppo pepper  
1 tablespoon kosher salt

**1** In a medium dry sauté pan over medium heat, lightly toast the cardamom pods, black peppercorns, coriander seeds, nigella seeds, and Aleppo pepper, starting with the largest spice first and gradually adding the others in order of decreasing size. Continue cooking, shaking the pan occasionally, until they're aromatic, 4 to 6 minutes total. Let cool completely. Transfer the spices and the salt to a spice grinder and grind to a coarse consistency. Keep in an airtight container for up to 3 months.

Fried Calamari with Spicy Sesame Syrup

Crispy Romaine Lettuce with Toasted Sesame Vinaigrette

Korean Slaw with Sesame

Buckwheat Noodles with Spiced Cashew Dressing

Burnt Rice Milkshake

Mustard Seed Relish

Cauliflower and Almond Purée

Spicy Peanut Butter Dressing

# Nutty 9

# Nutty | Going With My Gut

**I was raised by a father** who believed that there was a right way to do things. I went to school to learn the right way to cook. I've worked for amazing chefs who have taught me the right way to run a kitchen. But I've also learned that, in the end, there's never really just one right way. There's also that feeling in your gut, that instinctive belief in what's right for you even if it's not what everyone else thinks is right—and you have to listen to it.

After working for Jean-Georges and Ducasse, people said I shouldn't open a sandwich shop, that it didn't fit with my pedigree. But it was right for me. People said I shouldn't do a reality show, that it wasn't good for my reputation. But it was one of the best experiences of my life. Some people may think I shouldn't be making burgers and tacos, but hey, they're awesome burgers and tacos—and I'm having a great time doing it. It's taken me years to learn to follow my instincts, but one thing I know for sure: It's the only way I'm happy. The only way I feel true to myself is when I follow my heart.

Writing this book has been somewhat of a therapeutic process: Not only have I gotten to collect some of my favorite recipes together in one place (like organizing your closets—it's a great feeling to get all of it in order!), but I've also had the opportunity to think through the many stages of my life and to reflect on what I've done, why, and how it's turned out. Facing some of this stuff has been hard; I've had some dark moments along the way. Remembering some of it has made me laugh out loud. And some has been sweet and even brought me to the brink of tears. Overall, life so far has been incredibly gratifying—I've learned lessons, big and small, every step of the way. Mostly, looking back on all of it, I've learned that I have to nurture what's in front of me—right now. It's true what they say, that empires can rise and fall in a day, and you have to take care of what you have at this very moment because that's really all there is that you can be sure of—the present. Of course I'm still dreaming and planning for the future, but I know that enjoying and experiencing this moment is what it's all about.

I'm writing this book for my son. He's small now, but he's already had to face and overcome some serious medical challenges. I want him to know that he can do whatever he wants in life if he follows his heart and is passionate and dedicated. I want him to understand that while we don't have control over many of our circumstances—where we come from, who our parents are, how smart or talented we are—we do all have dreams and the power to follow those dreams, no matter where they lead. Our dreams are something no one else can define for us, and something no one should be able to take away, dismiss, or discourage.

I dreamt of being a chef, and with a lot of work, a great network of supporters, and a deep belief in myself, that dream came true. I decided that I was going to make it happen and I did—with all my heart. Sure, I may not have always done it the proverbial right way, but I did it the way that felt right for me. And I'm totally good with that.

# Fried Calamari with
# Spicy Sesame Syrup

**Serves: 4  Time: About 30 minutes  Flavors: Nutty/Sweet/Spicy**

I love eating with my hands—there's something very sensual about it—and calamari is the perfect finger food. Sure you're going to get a bit messy, a little sticky even with this spicy syrup, but it's worth it. I serve these tossed in a big bowl and drizzled with the sauce so everyone gets to dig in together and lick their fingers clean—definitely the best part.

**3 tablespoons sesame seeds**
**¼ cup all-purpose flour**
**2 tablespoons paprika**
**¼ cup soda water, chilled**
**grapeseed oil**
**¼ cup cornstarch**
**1 pound calamari, body cut into squares**
   **and tentacles left whole**
**1 lemon, cut into wedges**
**fresh cilantro leaves**

Spicy Sesame Syrup
**2 tablespoons grapeseed oil**
**2 tablespoons minced garlic**
**½ cup sugar**
**2 teaspoons kosher salt**
**¼ cup seasoned rice wine vinegar**
**¼ cup Sriracha sauce**
**2 tablespoons toasted sesame oil**

**1** In a dry medium sauté pan, lightly toast the sesame seeds over medium heat until just golden, about 2 minutes; set aside.

**2** Using the same pan, make the Spicy Sesame Syrup: Add the grapeseed oil and turn the heat to medium-high. Add the garlic and cook until it's just tender and aromatic, 2 to 3 minutes. Add the sugar and salt and stir to combine. Add the vinegar, Sriracha sauce, and sesame oil, bring to a simmer, and cook until the sugar has dissolved, about 2 minutes. Remove from the heat and let cool, then blend until smooth and set aside.

**3** In a large bowl, combine the flour, paprika, and soda water and mix until smooth. Refrigerate until ready to use.

**4** Pour enough oil into a large pot to come about 3 inches up the sides. Turn the heat to high and bring to 325°F, as measured by a deep-fry or candy thermometer. Meanwhile, line a sheet pan with paper towels and put it by the stove to hold the calamari as they come out of the oil.

**5** When the oil is hot, put the cornstarch in a medium bowl and toss the calamari in it to coat thoroughly, shaking off any excess. Once coated, dip the calamari in the soda water batter, again shaking off any excess. Fry the calamari, working in batches if necessary so you don't overcrowd the pan, until crisp and golden brown,

about 3 minutes. Using a slotted spoon, carefully remove the calamari from the oil and drain them on the prepared sheet pan.

**6** To serve, put the calamari in a large bowl, drizzle with the Spicy Sesame Syrup, sprinkle with the toasted sesame seeds, add a squeeze of fresh lemon, and garnish with the cilantro.

The key to really crisp fried food is maintaining an even temperature for the oil. If it gets too high the oil will burn and taste bitter; if it's too low you won't get that nice crisp exterior and your food will taste oily. I suggest using a deep-fry thermometer to monitor the heat—this calamari is too good to mess around with messed-up temps.

# Crispy Romaine Lettuce Salad
## with Toasted Sesame Vinaigrette

**Serves: 4    Time: About 20 minutes    Flavors: Nutty/Spicy/Earthy**

Toasted sesame oil has a very intense flavor, so a little goes a long way. When cooking with sesame oil, it's really important to remember to add it at the very end to maintain its integrity and prevent the flavor from turning bitter. Here the lemon juice and sugar tone down the pungency of the oil while still retaining the true essence of it.

½ cup lemon juice
2 tablespoons toasted sesame oil
3 tablespoons olive oil
3 tablespoons sugar
¼ teaspoon kosher salt
2 tablespoons gochujang paste
  (see Box, page 70)

4 cups romaine lettuce, chopped
½ cup sugar snap peas, cut in half
  diagonally
½ cup enoki mushrooms

**1** Combine the lemon juice, sesame oil, olive oil, sugar, salt, and gochujang paste in a blender and purée until smooth.

**2** Place the lettuce, snap peas, and mushrooms in a large bowl. Sprinkle with the salt, drizzle with the dressing, and toss well.

# Korean Slaw
# with Sesame

**Serves: 6   Time: About 45 minutes   Flavors: Nutty/Spicy/Floral**

In this recipe I only cure the cabbage for thirty minutes because I want the texture to reflect that wilted slaw-like consistency but still taste fresh. Add to this a bit of spice, a bit of toasted sesame oil, and the floral notes of the juniper berries and you've got a totally intriguing take on Korean cabbage. I like to serve it with hot dogs and hamburgers.

2 pounds green cabbage, shredded
¼ cup kosher salt
1 cup gochujang paste (see Box,
   page 70)
¼ cup toasted sesame oil

3 cups seasoned rice wine vinegar
1 cup sugar
4 star anise
6 juniper berries, cracked

**1** Put the cabbage in a large bowl, add the salt, toss well, and let sit for 30 minutes at room temperature. Rinse the cabbage in cold water and drain off all excess water (a salad spinner works well here). Set aside.

**2** Meanwhile, in another large bowl, combine the gochujang paste, sesame oil, vinegar, sugar, star anise, and juniper berries and stir well. Add the cabbage to the bowl, mix, and serve, or transfer to jars or other airtight containers and store in the fridge for up to 1 month.

# Buckwheat Noodles
# with Spiced Cashew Dressing

Serves: 4    Time: About 30 minutes    Flavors: Nutty/Spicy/Sweet

When it comes to these noodles, they're meant for slurping—don't be afraid to be heard across the table. Seriously. The cashew dressing is truly special—rich, nutty, and creamy—and it's followed by the refreshing pop of chilled sweet watermelon, which sort of explodes in your mouth and cleanses your palate. As far as I'm concerned, this is more than a meal—it's an experience.

Spicy Cashew Dressing
2 tablespoons grapeseed oil
2 tablespoons minced garlic
1 cup cashews
2 tablespoons sesame oil
¼ cup peanut butter
¼ cup gochujang paste (see Box, page 70)
2 tablespoons sugar

1 teaspoon salt
¼ cup water

1 pound buckwheat noodles
2 tablespoons grapeseed oil
¼ cup scallions, diagonally sliced
¼ cup fresh cilantro leaves
½ cup watermelon cubes

1 First make the Spicy Cashew Dressing: Heat the grapeseed oil in a medium saucepan over low heat. Add the garlic and sweat until just soft, about 2 minutes. Add the cashews and continue cooking for another 2 minutes, or until they are lightly toasted.

2 Add the sesame oil, peanut butter, gochujang paste, sugar, salt, and water; increase the heat to high, bring the mixture to a simmer, remove from the heat, and blend in a blender until smooth. Chill in the refrigerator for at least 20 minutes.

3 Fill a large pot with water and bring it to a boil. Add the noodles and cook until soft but still slightly firm in the middle. Drain in a colander and rinse under cold running water; transfer the noodles to a large bowl, toss them with the grapeseed oil to prevent them from sticking, and put them in the fridge for at least 20 minutes, until fully chilled.

4 Toss the chilled noodles with the Spicy Cashew Dressing; the noodles should be very wet. Serve the noodles garnished with the scallions, cilantro, and watermelon.

# Burnt Rice Milkshake

Serves: 4   Time: About 20 minutes   Flavors: Nutty/Sweet/Smoky

The idea here is to bring out the beautiful fragrance of the basmati rice by cooking it until the exterior is just charred; when you stop the cooking at this point, the interior retains a deep, toasty flavor. This technique adds an extra dimension to the rice by extracting its most aromatic essence. It's all about balance here—you want to take the rice to the edge and then pull it back before it goes too far.

1 cup basmati rice          3 cups whole milk
¼ cup sugar                 ½ cup ice

**1** In a medium sauté pan, toast the basmati rice to the point where the outside just darkens.

**2** Add the sugar to the pan. When the sugar begins to melt, add the milk, bring to a boil, and deglaze the pan.

**3** Remove the pan from the heat, pour everything into a blender, and pulse the mixture 3 or 4 times until the rice is coarsely ground. Strain the mixture through a fine-mesh sieve and chill for at least 20 minutes.

**4** When cool, add the ice and blend again until fine.

# Mustard Seed Relish

Makes: About 2 cups    Time: About 20 minutes
Flavors: Nutty/Sweet/Astringent

Just writing this recipe, my mouth is watering. The aromas of the popping mustard seeds and turmeric contrasted with the refreshing crunch of the peppers is just spectacular. Spread this on a hot dog or pastrami on rye and you're all set—it's a textural extravaganza.

3 tablespoons olive oil
½ cup mustard seeds
2 teaspoons ground turmeric
2 cups minced onions

1 cup diced green peppers
1 jalapeño chile, diced
½ cup sugar
½ cup seasoned rice wine vinegar

1 Put the oil in a medium saucepan over medium-high heat. When the oil is hot, add the mustard seeds and cook until they begin to pop, about 1 minute. Add the turmeric and cook for another 15 seconds. Reduce the heat to medium, add the onions, stir, and sweat for 5 minutes. Add the green peppers, jalapeño, and sugar and cook for another 3 minutes.

2 Increase the heat to high, add the vinegar, and cook until the liquid is reduced to just glazing the vegetables, about 3 minutes. Remove the pan from the heat, let cool, and use as desired, or transfer to an airtight container and refrigerate for up to 1 month.

# Cauliflower and Almond Purée

Serves: 6    Time: About 20 minutes    Flavors: Nutty/Sweet/Earthy

This is a phenomenal side dish that's beautiful with lamb, veal, or any red meat. Actually, it would be gorgeous with my Braised Short Ribs with Lemongrass Honey (page 30). It's very subtle and soft, so you can successfully pair it with Middle Eastern or Indian flavors.

2 pounds cauliflower, cut into florets
2 cups whole milk
3 cups water
1 cup blanched whole almonds

2 tablespoons unsalted butter
¼ cup sugar
1 teaspoon kosher salt

1 In a large saucepan, combine the cauliflower, milk, water, and almonds over medium-high heat. Bring to a boil and reduce the heat to medium; simmer for 10 minutes, or until the cauliflower is tender.

2 Carefully transfer the mixture to a blender or food processor (you may have to work in batches) and purée. Add the butter, sugar, and salt and blend until very smooth. Reheat if necessary before serving.

# Spicy Peanut
## Butter Dressing

**Makes: About 3 cups    Time: About 20 minutes    Flavors: Nutty/Sweet/Umami**

Want a simple dinner? Whip this up and toss it with buckwheat noodles and some fresh herbs and you're done. I like to add a chopped Asian pear to the mix for a crisp, refreshing textural twist. It also works brilliantly as a dipping sauce for satay, as a salad dressing, or doused over grilled chicken.

3 cups peanuts, chopped
2 tablespoons grapeseed oil
2 red Thai chiles, chopped
1 tablespoon grated ginger
1 tablespoon chopped garlic

3 cups coconut milk
3 tablespoons fish sauce
1 teaspoon kosher salt
2 tablespoons fresh lime juice

**1** Put the peanuts in a large saucepan over medium-high heat and toast for about 2 minutes, until just aromatic. Add the oil, chiles, ginger, and garlic and cook for another 2 minutes, or until the garlic just begins to color.

**2** Pour the coconut milk into the pan and, stirring frequently, allow it to reduce by about a third. Add the fish sauce and salt and cook for 2 more minutes.

**3** Remove the pan from the heat, add the lime juice, and let cool. Use immediately or store in an airtight container for up to 1 month.

# Index

# Acknowledgments

Every book has a beginning and an end, but the relationships that help bring the final result to life continue. These are the people who have joined me on my journey and who have helped make this book what it is.

To my amazing son Jacob: Right now you might not understand all the battles that you've faced, but I do. I wake up each morning thanking God that I have you in my life and striving to do all that I can to impact and inspire people the way that you have impacted and inspired me.

To my family: As the youngest, it brings me so much joy to share my stories of hard work, sacrifice, and success with all of you. You've all born witness to my struggles and you've stood alongside of me with unconditional support and love.

Aunt Carmen, as a young boy by your side at the stove, I couldn't have known how much you were influencing me. Now, sadly long after you're gone, I realize that it was you who inspired my life's passion—a passion found and nurtured in your kitchen. To this day you keep me grounded. Whenever I feel lost I know you're there with me; my true North Star.

I think all chefs must have mentors who help motivate them to grow, encourage them to excel, and give them the skills they need to be the best they can. Luckily I have had the benefit of the five of you: Alain Ducasse, Jean-Georges Vongerichten, Mark Hussey, Anthony Ligouri, Christian Bertrand.

To dream is one thing; to live the dream is another. As my team, I turn to you day in and day out to bring our dreams to life. You inspire me, challenge me, and believe in me. I think we're put on this earth to strive for greatness and with you beside me, I am convinced we will achieve it. Thank you Ricky Camacho, Jason Ezratty, Christopher Minnick, and Zach Minot.

Angela Miller, my agent, thank you for seeing something in me early on and encouraging me to share my passion for food and stories from my life. Anja Schmidt and Kyle Cathie, my editorial and publishing team, thank you for making this beautiful book exactly what I had hoped it would be. And thank you for bringing together a fantastic team, the people who made it look absolutely spectacular: William Brinson, Adrienne Anderson, Paige Hicks, and Nicky Collings.

To my co-author, Suzanne Lenzer, this book wouldn't be half of what it is if it wasn't for you and our connection. Your ability to listen and your approachable spirit allowed me to open up so that together we could put my stories and recipes on paper.

And lastly, to Katie, knowing that I have your support comforts me, encourages me, and makes me want to be more. Thank you.

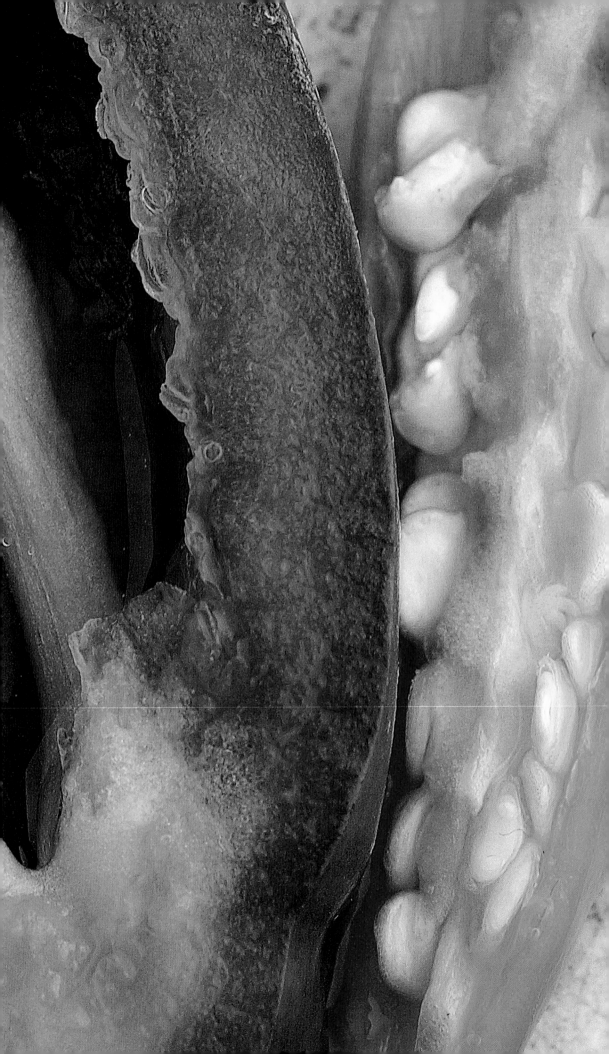